STAND UP
BECOMING FULLY ALIVE

The Early Christian Faith of Saint Irenaeus

DONNA SINGLES

STAND UP
Becoming Fully Alive
The Early Christian Faith of Saint Irenaeus
by
Donna Singles

Preface by
Ingmar Granstedt

Translated from French by
Danielle Gagneur and
Thomas Thomson

Edited by Elizabeth M. Reis, SSJ

ISBN #978-0-9820904-7-3
Center Space Publishing
32260 - 88th Avenue
Lawton, MI 49065

Book and Cover Design: Penny Kelly
Front Cover Photo: Philippe Grall
Iconographer: www.atelier-st-andré.net
Back Cover Photo: Keith de Cesare

Acknowledgments

Everyone needs a "nest" when working on a book such as Sister Donna Singles' powerful theological insight and reflection on St. Irenaeus' faith within the Apostolic Church of Lyon, France, during the mid second century. The following people and groups are those who helped create that nest – a safe place to work, rest, and grow with a view to the publication of Donna Singles' book in English.

* Sister Barbara Kennison, who returned to France to help a very sick Sister Donna Singles close her ministry center and say good-bye to a forty-year collection of beloved friends, colleagues, and students. Barbara has been the faithful 'bridge' between Donna and her community.

* The Sisters of St. Joseph, who lived and worked at Nazareth, Michigan and who covered us with prayer, encouragement, and enthusiasm as we launched the prospect of the publication in English.

* The translators, Danielle Gagneur and Thomas Thomson, who volunteered to translate Donna Singles' book from French into English in order to make her work and Irenaeus' faith accessible to an American audience and first and foremost to the sisters of the congregation. A faithful translation based on a thorough study of the text and enlightening comments on the translating process. A volunteer work completed by the will to submit and share their work with the Sisters of the Congregation, which led them to travel from France to Nazareth, Michigan USA.

* Marylin Nichols who triggered the reflection on the use of the word "man" when commenting on the first choice of the title as *Man Fully Alive*. "Why not use the word *human* instead?" she asked, bringing up the type of concern that led, for instance, to a new translation of *The Phenomenon of Man* by Teilhard de Chardin into *The Human Phenomenon*, a question that the translators of Donna Singles' book took up seriously.

* The Nazareth employees who fed, served, and welcomed our team of six during the days we lived and worked at Nazareth.

* Barbara Gourley, who typed this Acknowledgement during her own lunch time and time after work - something only God could have inspired.

* The four Sisters of St. Joseph, lovingly called GREM (an acronym composed of the first letters of their names) who offered their own unique skills to the process – skills necessary to smooth out the translation and create the kind of flow needed for an ordinary American reader:

    Sr. Grace Scola
    Sr. Mary Rene Poirier
    Sr. Elizabeth M. Reis
    St. Mila Sones

* Penny Kelly, responsible for copy-editing, book design, and publishing the book, without whom all this work would not have come to life in the USA.

TABLE OF CONTENTS

Preface

ACCORDING TO SAINT IRENAEUS, THE VOCATION OF HUMAN BEINGS is inscribed in their flesh fashioned in God's image. For Donna Singles, who was a student of theology in Lyon, that statement came as a real shock at the time she heard it pronounced by Professor Maurice Jourjon. Eighteen centuries lie between us, yet the thoughts of Irenaeus are so close to the sources of the Christian faith that they can still speak to men and women of our time through his joyful vision of the advent of Christ, his view of life as a growing process and his call upon us to participate in the unfinished symphony of creation.

Donna Singles came to Lyon from the USA, her native land, and it was in Lyon, the capital of the Gauls, that Irenaeus settled after leaving Smyrna, his native town (now Izmir in Turkey). Their similar faiths met across the centuries, thus spurring for years the considerable energy and enthusiasm of this exceptional American woman.

Combining passion with precision and the mastery born of her long studies of Irenaeus' work, Donna offers us here her 'key for reading,' a reader's guide to access Irenaeus' language which is that of the early centuries, in order to discover how clearly he can speak to us and enlighten our lives today. The chapters of the book quite simply follow the articles of the Creed, the Apostles' Creed, Irenaeus' own faith being utilized as a way of throwing light on each of the articles. This provides a particularly clear and accessible presentation.

The author, Donna Singles was born in 1928 in Grand Rapids, Michigan. She entered the Congregation of the Sisters of Saint Joseph when she was twenty, and then became a teacher in their schools. In 1967 she came to France to study theology at the Catholic University of Lyon, which led to her doctoral thesis, "Le Salut de l'homme chez saint Irénée. Essai d'interprétation symbolique." (*The Salvation of Humanity according to Saint Irenaeus. A Study in Symbolic Interpretation*).

She stayed in this university where she then became a full member of the teaching staff. She lectured on Irenaeus, of course, but also conducted study groups and courses on the Eucharist, ministry and hope, as well as an important, though little known movement in France, referred to as 'process theology,' a way of conceiving God as continuously becoming. This was the work of the mathematician and philosopher A. N. Whitehead, whose major work, *Process and Reality*, was published in 1929 [1]. Sister Donna Singles also took part in a multidisciplinary study group on the neurosciences and wrote articles in magazines such as *Concilium, Echanges, Golias, Lumière et vie, Unité chrétienne* and others.

Listening to the convictions "surging from the depths of her being," she "was proud to be a woman, without sex rivalry or obsession with equal rights", says her friend Henri Denis, for whom she worked for a while as an assistant. She took part in the feminist movement within the Catholic Church, convinced that the current awakening of women was theologically justified and that it would have important positive consequences. She devoted her skills to help

---

[1] Translated into French in 1995 with the title, *Procès et réalité. Un essai de cosmologie*, Published by Gallimard.

organizations, in particular the resource center of "Femmes et Christianisme" and was in contact with women theologians in Europe. With Renée Dufour and Marie Jeanne Bérère, she published in 1982 *Et si on ordonnait des femmes…? What if Women Were Ordained…?* [2]

Still listening to the inner voice of her conscience in the light of faith, Donna committed herself in the critical movement against Roman authoritarianism, especially in the last ten years of her life.

With her thirst for freedom and justice, she kept herself well-informed about social and political changes in the USA to which she felt strongly bonded, as well as to her congregation. She helped her French friends to see the face of America which she loved, an America far removed from that of money and power, the America that believed itself to be *the* nation blessed by God.

Donna Singles loved life, enjoyed cooking and good wine. She was happy to welcome people to her table in her small cluttered flat. She led groups in bible study, played the piano and, as a good photographer, she knew how to capture the beauty of nature. Every week she used to go to the cinema to get a feel for contemporary issues.

When her meager income allowed, she went traveling with friends. All these aspects of her love of life were, for her, opportunities for convivial social interaction and deep contacts through which she made true friends, as she valued friendship most highly. For example, she went to Berlin for a week to stay with an American friend who was dying of AIDS.

It is not surprising that a person with such a love of life, such a thirst for liberty and justice – a fully alive woman – should have

---

2 *Et si on ordonnait des femmes …?*, Marie–Jeanne Bérère, Renée Dufourt, Donna Singles, Editions du Centurion, 1982. Paris.

been drawn to Saint Irenaeus who said, "The glory of God is man fully alive; and the life of man is the vision of God."

She still had a project dear to her heart which was to make Irenaeus' belief, his grasp and joyous expression of the Christian faith, known to a wider audience. But, cancer which she had overcome three times in her lifetime, with the zest for life which was so typical of her, was finally to carry her away.

Just before she died, in January 2005, she gave me her documents, asking me to take over the rest of the work with a view to publication. Deeply moved by her trust in me, I accepted. I knew what she had in mind having talked to me about it long before. In her documents I found a clear and detailed outline with all the chapters already written. For some of them, there were several successive versions with different emphases which required choice. I made these choices, while being as faithful as possible to her vision, with a concern for the overall coherence, while making a few stylistic alterations. The text of this posthumous book is thus truly Donna's work.

I am happy that her work and enthusiasm for Saint Irenaeus of Lyon, whose theology conveys such pure joy, may now be known to the public. It is up to the readers to seek here food for their faith and hope.

INGMAR GRANSTEDT

Foreword

IRENAEUS, THE SECOND BISHOP OF LYON, IS VIEWED AS THE FIRST great theologian of the Church. He was a scholar, not a bookworm confined to his study. Above all he was a pastor, a man of faith, close to the small Christian community in Lyon at the end of the second century.

Still more significant for us, Irenaeus was very close to the sources of faith. He said so himself when speaking about his childhood in Smyrna in Asia Minor where he had been instructed in the catechism by the old bishop Polycarp whom he considered the disciple of John the Apostle. This means he is the third link in the chain between the people baptized in his time and Jesus himself. When we read Irenaeus, we discover the way Christians received and lived the Gospel only a few generations after the final compiling of the New Testament.

The writings of Irenaeus can speak directly to a reader today because there is something strikingly modern about them, but also because they direct us systematically back to the sources of the Gospel which, one way or another, address our own problems of faith. This return to the origins is essential as it makes possible a fresh or a renewed outlook on faith. It can fortify in us this wonderful understanding or grasp of faith that Vatican II referred to as "sensus fidelium," thanks to which we are deeply sensitive to the truth of the faith. Not only does this understanding support us in our progress as believers, but also it can enlighten us as to the evangelical way of meeting the needs of the community.

In order to have access to the way Irenaeus thought, I shall take one by one the articles of the *Apostles' Creed*, the 'short' Creed as we say it at Mass, and see, through Irenaeus' work, the way he understood and lived them. A chapter will be devoted to each article of the Creed.

Yet even before that, it would be better to start with a few pages about the life of Irenaeus in his historical context.

CHAPTER 1

IRENAEUS IN HIS CONTEXT IN THE SECOND CENTURY

IT IS NOT EASY TO WRITE A BIOGRAPHY OF THE SECOND BISHOP of Lyon, because we know so little about his life. We have a few glimpses thanks to Eusebius of Caesarea who died in 340. In his Ecclesiastical History,[3] Eusebius refers to "The Letter of the Martyrs of Lyon" (177), the Easter controversy, and the publication of *Against Heresies* when Eleutherius was the bishop of Rome (175-189). With these sparse chronological references and with a great deal of guesswork, historians have tried to put together the life of Irenaeus.

FROM SMYRNA TO LYON

What we get from these few bibliographical elements is that Irenaeus was right at the crossroads of the Church of his time. He was probably born between 130 and 140 in Smyrna, Asia Minor, what is now Izmir in Turkey. According to tradition and to Irenaeus himself, this town is always associated with Polycarp, the disciple of

---

3 Eusebe de Cesaree, *Histoire ecclésiastique*, V, Paris, ED du Cerf, coll. «Sources chrétiennes », n° 41, 1955.

the apostle John. In the second century, Rome and Asia Minor were the two major centers of Christianity. Smyrna was a flourishing, prosperous city because of its merchants who went as far as to sail up the Rhône to sell their products. This probably accounts for the fact that there was an important settlement of Middle Eastern Christians in the city of Lyon located at the junction of the Saône and the Rhône.

Perhaps this may also account for what seems to be a very early presence of Christians in this city. Smyrna seemed to have significantly important links with Rome. Young provincials used to try their luck in the capital in order to learn from the famous masters of the time and in the famous schools in Rome. There were also, in Rome, institutions that taught the Christian doctrine. Later on, these were to become theological schools – Smyrna in the East, Rome and Lyon in the West. The life of Irenaeus took place between these two worlds, that of the East and that of the West.

Born in the East, Irenaeus was probably baptized when he was very young. "The purity and the resolve of his faith indicate that he was not a pagan convert, but was from a family who had been Christian for a long time." [4] Anyway, Irenaeus himself spoke of the catechism he was taught by Polycarp when he was still young.

It is also thanks to Eusebius that we have a letter Irenaeus wrote to his former classmate, Florinus. Irenaeus recalls his memory of the venerable Bishop Polycarp, referring to him as a spiritual father whom he liked very much. It is tempting to quote a great deal of this letter because it tells us a lot about Irenaeus himself – about his pastoral dimension, about his faith, and his way of dealing with people outside the church. This letter shows something very characteristic about Irenaeus. He always tries to lead the person with

---

4   A. Benoit, *Saint Irénée. Introduction à l'étude de sa théologie*, Paris, PUF, 1960, p. 9.

whom he is dealing to the point where he or she is ready to learn. He constantly tries to have the other person open his or her mind to accept the faith of the apostles willingly and enthusiastically.

This is Irenaeus writing to his childhood friend:

I saw you, indeed, when I was still a child, in Asia Minor, with Polycarp: you shone out at the imperial court and you were doing your best to make a name for yourself in his eyes. For I remember what happened then, better than recent events. In fact, knowledge acquired in childhood grows with the soul and unites with it, so that I can tell you where the blessed Polycarp used to sit to speak, the way he came and went, his way of life, his physical appearance, his talks in front of the crowd, the way he spoke of his relationship with John and those who had seen the Lord, the way he quoted their words and what he had heard them say about the Lord, His miracles, His teaching; the way, after having been given all this by the eye witnesses to the Living Word, Polycarp told about this in accordance with the Scriptures. These things too, by the grace of God bestowed upon me, I have listened to them carefully, and I have recorded them not on paper but in my heart, and still by the grace of God I have thought about these things faithfully, and I can assert in the sight of God, that if that blessed apostolic presbyter [Polycarp] had heard something similar (to what you are saying, Florinus) he would have cried out and stopped up his ears...

Maurice Jourjon commented on this letter to express what the Church meant for Irenaeus:

For Irenaeus, the Church transmitted the faith... For him, as for the Church, what mattered was seeding the Gospel truth in the hearts of the very young like a tree which would grow with them, so that their whole life would be bathed in its light. This confidence speaks volumes. His tone, so perfectly attuned to what we think or feel after centuries of

Christianity, is not all…What Irenaeus learned, when he was young, is a life, a story of salvation which was part of his own life.[5]

What can be said factually about Irenaeus' life? He must have left his family like many other youths from Asia Minor, to learn from masters in many different capitals of the Roman Empire. His writings show that he had a good general education, without seeking to become a scholar in one of the schools of the time. His knowledge of the Bible was very thorough. One is struck by the number of times that quotations seemed to come to him naturally when he wanted to highlight a teaching point.

It is believed that Irenaeus spent some time in Rome itself, perhaps with Saint Justin who had founded a school of Christian doctrine in the capital. Why then did he come to Lyon? We do not know but it was perhaps to join the young Church, which was beginning to take shape thanks to the presence of a number of his fellow countrymen in the city.

The origins of the Church of Lyon are not clear. It seems that the first Christians of Lyon came from Rome at the beginning of the second century. For Lyon, like the other cities of the Empire, the Gospel came with the Roman conquest, by means of its road and river transport networks. The city of Lyon undoubtedly played a major part in the early stages of European Christianity. Historically, the town was the door through which the Gospel came from the Mediterranean basin into the continent of Europe, and because of the Eastern origin of a great number of the Baptized in Lyon, we can think of it as a genuine bridge between two civilizations, between the two major areas of the Church, the West and the East.

---

5 M. Viller et al. (dir.), *Dictionnaire de spiritualité ascétique et mystique*, Paris, Beauchesne, 1932-1995, t. IV, p. 405.

In any case, Irenaeus lived in the city of Lyon in 177 when the persecution of the Christians broke out. Eusebius said Irenaeus was already a 'presbyter.' At the time of Irenaeus, this word did not yet have a precise meaning. In several of Irenaeus' writings, 'presbyter' is synonymous with 'bishop,' hence, there are several interpretations. One is that after the death of Pothinus, the first bishop of Lyon and a victim of the persecution, Irenaeus had already been appointed as the second bishop (or presbyter) when the Christians of Lyon gave him letters to take to Eleutherius, the bishop of Rome. The second interpretation is that the authors of the letters to Eleutherius were asking the bishop of Rome to acknowledge Irenaeus as a presbyter, in some way or other to ordain him bishop. There is nothing that would allow us to validate or invalidate either of these interpretations. One thing is certain, when he came back from Rome, Irenaeus was viewed as the successor of Pothinus, which meant he was the only bishop of Gaul. If we believe what Eusebius said, "Irenaeus writes in the name of his brothers as their leader in Gaul."

Eusebius was the one who referred to a particularly valuable testimony from the Christians of Lyon when they requested the bishop of Rome to grant him audience. "We have asked our brother and companion Irenaeus, to give you these letters, and we are asking you to view him as a champion of the will of Christ. Given the circumstances, had anybody insisted, we might have referred to him as a presbyter of the Church, which he is in fact."

Irenaeus, having become the second bishop after the death of the old bishop Pothinus in prison, was not only in charge of his own Church, but also strove for peace between the churches.

He wrote letters to individuals and to church officials about doctrinal and disciplinary issues. In this respect, we think above all about the controversy over the date of Easter which broke out while he was a bishop.

Eusebius tells at great length of the controversy in which Irenaeus was to play an important part. For a long time, Eastern and Western Christians had been divided over the celebration of the Easter festival and over the different ways of fasting before the festival. They seemed to be getting along fine with this. In 190, Victor, the bishop of Rome, brought the issue to a head. Perhaps he was irritated by the Christians who had come to Rome from the four corners of the Empire and who had retained their former liturgical practices. Eastern Christians, in accordance with Jewish custom, dated Easter from the first full moon after the fourteenth of Nisan. In fact, this meant that they began to celebrate, to break Lent, while their neighbors of the Roman Church were still fasting. Victor thus decided to excommunicate all those who did not celebrate the Resurrection on Sunday, that is to say, in accordance with the practice of the Roman Christians.

Irenaeus clearly saw the danger presented by Victor's decision. Hence, he wrote to the bishop of Rome, asking him to distinguish between what was essential and what was not. For Irenaeus what mattered above all was the unity of the Faith – precisely reinforced by the diversity of customs. Insisting on the fact that Christians, in the past, remained at peace amongst themselves despite the diversity of their customs, he said "the difference (in observing) the fast establishes the harmony of (our common) faith." [6] Eusebius, telling of this event, closes his account with a very significant comment:

Irenaeus was worthy of his name, because he was a peacemaker by name and by his behavior. This is how he preached and argued

____

6 Eusebe de Cesaree, *Histoire ecclésiastique*, V, p.70.

for peace between the Churches. He communicated by letters not only with Victor but also with a very large number of Church leaders, about communities concerning issues over which they were debating. Pastor and man of peace, Irenaeus was also a writer, precisely in order to fulfill his pastoral role as bishop and not for the sake of debate.

An Emerging Church in Crisis

In order to understand Irenaeus' writings, one needs to put them into context. A writer's work inevitably depends on the circumstances in which it is produced. This is particularly true in the case of Irenaeus.

From his writings, we know that at the core of his thinking and of his pastoral work, his major concern was to maintain unadulterated the tradition handed down from the Apostles. This meant above all, that the Resurrection was to be held before the eyes of the faithful as the central tenet of the apostolic tradition. Today, we find it very difficult to conceive the degree of incredulity but also of hope aroused by the idea that God had raised a human being from the dead and glorified him by having him at His right hand as the Savior of humanity. The first to hear this stated must have seen it as something strange, even insane (as shown in the first chapter of Acts). But, we also know that the belief in the Risen Christ crossed the Roman Empire with stunning speed to become *the* major undeniable reference point for an emerging church trying to find her way.

The tenacity with which the early Christians maintained their belief in the Resurrection, as their source of unity among themselves, is all the more surprising as it came from very scattered and diverse communities. Indeed, in terms of church organization, the authorities responsible for unity were not yet specified. There was an ecclesiastical 'fluidity' because the very faith of the Baptized was the guarantor of the unity between the different local churches scattered throughout the Roman Empire.

If one looks back at the origins of Christianity, one must admit that it would take several centuries for the Church to move away from this ecclesiastical flexibility by seeking to normalize, to codify, and even to 'Romanize' the local Churches. It thus provided them with a two-speed structure consisting of a triple hierarchy, deacon-priest-bishop on the one hand, and a people submitted to its authority on the other.

However, at the time of Irenaeus, this point had not yet been reached. As we have just seen, the life of Christian communities did not depend on an ecclesiastical hierarchy but essentially on the quality of the faith of their members.

This accounts for one of Irenaeus' main concerns, that is to say, the need to strengthen the Baptized in their faith in the Resurrection. At the end of the second century, their faith ran the risk of being undermined by different groups and movements. These denied the Church as a way to salvation and replaced the *ecclesia*-community with all kinds of personal or individual spiritual formulae, all claiming to provide their followers with the means of their own salvation without the mediation of a risen Savior. Indeed, in Irenaeus' time, everything was in flux: omens of an Empire in agony, sects swollen with disillusioned or bewildered Christians, persecutions breaking out without warning almost everywhere. In a word, the Church was in utter crisis as Irenaeus showed when speaking of Christians who had left the Church hoping to find salvation elsewhere, for instance, with one or other of the charismatic gurus crisscrossing the Rhône valley.

Indeed, when reading Irenaeus, it can be said that the provisory nature of the Church of the time made him a man in a hurry to explain the essential components of faith. Thus, his major work written around 180, *On the Detection and Overthrow of the So-Called Gnosis*, commonly called *Against Heresies,* was an attempt to persuade the Christians lured by sects to question with honesty and intelligence their reasons for deserting the Church. Irenaeus did not condemn them nor resort to arbitrary authority, but called on them to use their common sense and reasoning ability. In other words, if he demonstrated, refuted, and denounced the weakness of the Gnostic teaching of the gurus, he did not blame the Christians who sincerely let themselves be won over. For Irenaeus, the threat that the Gnostics posed for the baptized Christians lay in the lack of arguments to expose their deceptive doctrine.

The way Irenaeus went about this was to suggest a deeper understanding of the nature of faith. He was confident in the fact that those who wanted to be called true Christians would not be fooled.

The word *Gnosis* may need some explanation. It refers to a complex and very widespread phenomenon in the second century. It consisted of a mixture of various sets of beliefs and spiritual theories claiming to bring salvation to their followers by an access to knowledge restricted to the elect – for instance, the secret knowledge of the so-called hidden words of Jesus.

If Irenaeus addressed the baptized Christians seduced by Gnosis with benevolence, he showed anger at those he considered as hypocritical or insincere, i.e. the 'illuminated' who were causing so much disruption amongst Christians. (For that matter, it would be interesting to see if there are not commonalities between the second-century Gnosis and some current spiritual searches such as New Age, reincarnation, fusion in the Great Whole, transcendental meditation, participation in cosmic energy, Eastern mysticism, recourse to mediums, etc.)

Who were the Gnostics? What caused Irenaeus to write against them? All this is very complex because Gnosis is not a phenomenon restricted to the second century. We cannot even talk about Gnosis in the singular but about Gnoses in the plural – esoteric ways of thinking that were very widespread in the East at the time of Irenaeus but which seemed to have begun long before Christianity. If the various Gnostic belief systems which were spreading throughout the Roman Empire and Gaul cannot be considered as identical, they had at least one thing in common: they all claimed to provide a secret 'knowledge' by means of which their followers were saved. Sometimes they seem to have been made up entirely from the most heterogeneous borrowings from paganism, Judaism, and Christianity. It is precisely this esotericism that makes them so extremely complex and difficult to analyze.

Gnosis had a great deal of success amongst religious people at the time of Irenaeus, including many Christians. It drew on very human feelings particularly relevant at the time of Irenaeus – the wish to know with certainty what we are, where we come from, and where we are going. The second-century Roman Empire was especially affected by the phenomenon of religious disquiet, by the anxiety that manifested itself in the multiplication of sects. These sects were characterized – to a greater or lesser extent – by secret initiations, magical practices, and teachings that evoked the ancient mysteries of paganism. They were wonderfully suited to people's woes. Claiming that humans were incapable of knowing happiness here below, the sects taught a contempt for the material world and that of the flesh. It was thus in this essentially pessimistic atmosphere that the key position of the Gnostics took shape.

For instance, Valentinus, a Christian living in Rome, had conceived a grandiose and complex cosmological vision, based on the dualist principle of an irreconcilable opposition between flesh and spirit. According to him and his followers, only a certain number of the privileged were intended to have access to the divine world because of their very nature as 'spiritual' beings. Thanks to a personal and inner experience of enlightenment, these privileged ones were to become aware of a divine spark within themselves. This awareness was expressed in terms of a secret knowledge or 'gnosis' leading them to find out that God was the true cause of their being. Consequently, they viewed themselves in this world as manifestations of a divine source, which accounts for their deep conviction of being exiled from their true homeland of divine plenitude. The spark of light, locked in the very depths of their soul, thus filled them with an unquenchable desire to go back to their divine origin. In the meantime, they prepared themselves by contemplation, ascetic exercises, purifications and the renunciation of the pleasures of the flesh. They somehow behaved as 'God's sporting champions.'

A great many Christians considered this the key to spirituality in the middle of the second century. For them, Christ was a timeless being who, in this world, had only taken on the appearance of a man called Jesus in order to teach the chosen – and only the chosen – about their true nature. The spiritual component borne in their soul made them 'strangers to this world,' just like the transcendental God onto whom they projected their nostalgia for a Hereafter. A Gnostic devoted all his energy to denying matter and time, which he considered as a *place of exile*; hence, his need to escape from this despicable and worthless world in order to become more and more *spiritual* or *pneumatic*.

Irenaeus, The First Theologian
of the Church

When Irenaeus attacked the Gnostics, his main concern was their concept of salvation. All Gnostic belief systems are based on a common denominator, a secret knowledge which can lead only the initiates to salvation.

The core of this knowledge can be put in two words – *Know Thyself*. The Gnostic does not need to believe; he knows. He knows himself by knowing his true self, his essential self, whom he thinks of in terms of a divine seed or a spark of life locked into his body. The Gnostic thinks of himself essentially as a spiritual being, a spirit provisionally clothed in a body from which he must set himself free. His salvation is to be found precisely in the knowledge that he has been given about his true nature.

Thanks to this knowledge, a Gnostic can reach the upper world from whence he came. In other words, Gnostic salvation is not *reconciliation* but the reuniting of the divine spark with the supreme One. Hence, a Gnostic has no need of a savior but of knowledge transmitted to the initiates.

So, what is to be done to confront these attractive ideas? Above all, Irenaeus thought it necessary to debunk the cosmological concept that was the starting point of the Gnostic belief systems – the idea that the divine seed locked into a spiritual being is a part of divinity itself. It is something that is not created but which emanates directly from the divine. It is precisely this principle of emanation that is at the core of Gnostic cosmologies and that defines the relationship between the spiritual and the material worlds in terms of opposition, even antagonism. One of these belief systems, taught by Marc le Mage, is explained in detail by Irenaeus in his first book, *Against Heresies*. Marc asserted the existence of a supreme God beyond the Jewish God in the Old Testament. This unknown God, the perfect Father, was not responsible for the creation of the world that is evil. Very much the opposite! Marc insisted that creation was the work of the Demiurge, the evil God of the Old Testament. As for the perfect God, He remained beyond all knowledge and was only revealed to the spiritual. As for the others, the carnal and the psychic, they are doomed from the start.

It is this cosmology that Irenaeus sought to refute: the pessimistic view totally contrary to the universal message delivered by Christ. This is what accounts for his great piece of work, *Against Heresies,* in which he was led to unmask the Gnostic myth of the origins of the world and of humanity.

But, these attacks against Gnosis are not what make Irenaeus a theologian. What is rather extraordinary and unexpected is that Irenaeus gradually moved away from polemics!

He was led to go much further than he thought he would at first, and gradually his vision turned into a true presentation of the Christian faith. He constantly referred to the sources of Christianity, to the faith handed down by the churches since the Apostles. This is how he became a true Christian thinker and theologian. We thus understand why later generations of Christians referred to him as the first theologian of the Church. F. Vernet writes, "Irenaeus is the first writer of the post-apostolic times worthy of the title of theologian. By the richness of his doctrine as well by the direction he gave to theology, Irenaeus is indeed the great name of the history of dogma, between Saint Paul and Saint John on the one hand and Saint Augustine on the other." [7]

---

7 *Dictionnaire de théologie catholique*, Paris, Letouzey et Ané, 1927, VII, col. 2533, article « Irénée ».

The century of Irenaeus, which is sometimes referred to as "The Spring of the Church" – because everything seemed possible – was also full of dangers for Christians who experienced not only the joy of faith, but also the hardships that it entailed. Irenaeus was well aware of this, hence his efforts to preserve the integrity of the faith by providing it with solid foundations.

How long did he live? We do not know exactly. We know neither the date nor the circumstances of the death of the first theologian of the Church. Perhaps he died during the reign of Septimius Severus (192-211)? As a martyr? This is what some traditions claim, but they appeared later.

Now we shall find out how Irenaeus understood and lived the Christian faith. The articles of the *Creed*, the *Apostles' Creed*, will be our milestones in this journey of discovery. ■

CHAPTER II

I Believe in God, The Father Almighty, Creator of Heaven and Earth

Confronted by successive political and social crises in the Roman Empire of the second century, people were seeking reassurance – and this they found in the Gnostic theories. The elected, the followers of the Gnostic belief systems, thought that by rejecting the material world and escaping into the spiritual, thanks to secret knowledge given by a guru through initiatory rites, they could be reunited with what they thought was their Origin.

Irenaeus well understood the danger of such ideas for Christians drawn to Gnosis. The Gnostics implicitly denied the 'epiphanic' dimension of creation and its capacity or aptitude to be the place for the manifestation of God since he viewed it as a consequence of corruption, as a place of exile. In other words, for the Gnostic, creation had nothing to do with salvation, and consequently with Incarnation, Redemption, and the Resurrection of the flesh. If Irenaeus sought to win over the Christians seduced by Gnosis, he was thus obliged to respond vigorously. This he did initially by attacking the Gnostic pessimism towards the material world and creation.

CREATION IS AN UNFINISHED SYMPHONY

In order to refute the Gnostic idea that humans do not belong to this world, Irenaeus insisted on the fact that they find salvation on this earth. According to Gnostics, a human being is a fallen being, who has fallen into the mud. Thrown into the world as an exile, a human is a stranger who has to find salvation by escaping the world where he does not belong.

Against this profoundly pessimistic view, Irenaeus opposes Saint Paul's doctrine of recapitulation in all things, of the whole cosmos in Christ. "He revealed to us the mystery of His will...in order to unite (recapitulate) all things in Christ." (Ep. 1:10) Saint Irenaeus' commentary on Ephesians 1:10 is the finest that we have from Classical times. Everything is to be united in Christ, including the material world, since it is the work of God made by Him according to His will, "And this great created world, prepared by God before the formation of man, was given to man as his place, containing all things within itself." (Dem. 11) [8]

In Irenaeus' eyes, it was logical that God should have prepared a beautiful and good place for humans to have a worthy dwelling during their time on earth. The Lord made this prodigious work of creation, their future home, not with the help of an inferior god or angels but with His own Hands – by the Word and the Spirit of

---

8   – (Dem.11) standing for *Demonstration of the Apostolic Preaching*, Paragraph 11.

   – English quotes are taken from J. Armitage Robinson's translation of Irenaeus *The Proof/Demonstration of the Apostolic Preaching*, www.tertullian.org/fathers/irenaeus.

   – Donna Singles used *Démonstration de la prédication apostolique* (traduit de l'arménien par L.-M. Froidevaux, Paris, ED du Cerf, coll. "Sources chrétiennes", 1971.

creation. This has nothing to do with a world born of ignorance or corruption. Irenaeus is adamant on this point as he knows that only a creation that belongs to God can sustain and recognize His own Lord in the very person of the Incarnate Word, *"For indeed the creation could not have sustained Him (on the cross), if He had sent forth (simply by commission) what was the fruit of ignorance and defect... How could that creation which was concealed from the Father, and far removed from Him, have sustained His Word?" (A.H. Bk V, 18: 1)*[9]

The world is thus fundamentally good as it is stated in Genesis. It is the work of Wisdom and divine power, not something derived from pre-existing chaos. This stress on *ex nihilo* creation by Irenaeus is linked to his theology. What Irenaeus is interested in is not so much the physical and material origin of the world as the idea that, regardless of its origin, the world is the manifestation of a free God. God is Himself involved with His own Hands in His creation. The universe is the manifestation of Wisdom and the *Son*, that is to say, the *Spirit and the Word*. Irenaeus never loses sight of the fact that they both take part in creation. Thanks to the power of the Word, the universe has been established; thanks to the Breath of the Father, things exist in all their might. In this, Irenaeus follows the Bible, according to which everything is because of the creative Word of the Father (the Word) and everything is filled with creative dynamism because of the Spirit. One of the consequences of this theology is that

---

9 - (A.H. Bk V, 18:1) standing for *Against Heresies*, Book V, Chapter 18, Paragraph 1.

    - English quotes are taken from *Against Heresies* by St. Irenaeus, Fathers of the Church, www.newadvent.org, translated by Alexander Roberts and William Rambaut. From *Ante-Nicene Fathers, Vol. 1.* Edited by Alexander Roberts, James Donaldson, and A. Cleveland Coxe. (Buffalo, NY; Christian Literature Publishing Co, 1885.) Revised and edited for New Advent by Kevin Knight, www.newadvent.org.

    - Donna Singles used the French translation from *Contre les hérésies* (*Contre les hérésies. Dénonciation et réfutation de la prétendue gnose au nom menteur,* traduction Fse Adelin Rousseau, Paris, ED du Cerf, 1991, 3rd Edition).

there is no continuity between the world and its Creator other than the gift of divine words of wisdom, that is to say, that which is at the core of an intelligent being. This means that creation is radically different from the divine, like everything which we make. Its coherence and unity are not due to an emanation from (or degradation of) the Divine, but they derive from a free and personal act of the Divine Artist who, Himself, is at work in the world with both His Hands, the Word, and the Wisdom, while he is supporting the work of humans.

This approach has another consequence. Such a God is not a distant God; He is very close to His creation. The image of the *Hands of God* gives Irenaeus a means to clarify a very important tenet of the faith of the Apostles, namely that creation is meant to be for the salvation of humanity. With this image Irenaeus evokes not only the ease with which God created the world, but also His caring attitude towards His creation.

The Word and the Wisdom (the Spirit) have fashioned all things with loving care; they have established them as beings in their own right, *"Now God shall be glorified in His handiwork, fitting it so as to be conformable to, and modeled after, His own Son. For by the hands of the Father, that is, by the Son and the Holy Spirit, man, and not (merely) a part of man, was made in the likeness of God."* (A.H. Bk V, 6: 1)

However, this care does not cease when this work is done because Irenaeus insists on the fact that *the Hands of God* are themselves involved in the task of bringing His creation towards its fulfillment. All things, from the beginning to the end, are brought to their perfection, *"the Son, administering all things for the Father, works from the beginning even to the end, and without Him no man can attain the knowledge of God."* (A.H. Bk IV, 6: 7)

The dynamic theme of fulfillment made possible through created things is particularly important to Irenaeus. It is to be found everywhere. The idea of *creation as a process* is consistent with that of a human viewed essentially as a growing being (as we shall see further on). The image of the Hands of God therefore evokes the effort and the patience of the craftsman who indefatigably carries on his work so that the results reflect faithfully the idea that inspired him. This same image evokes the link between the artist and his work, that is to say, the intimacy – even cooperation – in which the raw material lets itself be shaped by its master's hands.

The Hands of God also do things in harmony. This word *harmony* immediately triggers Irenaeus' image of the 'symphony' or of the melody of creation. Humans must listen to the melody of creation in order to be able to sing a song of thanksgiving to God for having created for them such a varied, and at the same time, organized world.

The image of the symphony of creation is especially enlightening with respect to the question of suffering. The work of creation has not yet been completed. This is why 'dissonances' cannot be avoided. A world of such diversity and richness, full of energy and growth, inevitably implies discords and conflict. This is what Irenaeus says, "*...created things are various and numerous, they are indeed well fitted and adapted to the whole creation; yet, when viewed individually, are mutually opposite and inharmonious...*" (A.H. Bk II, 25: 2) The harmony of the world does not exclude discord between the various elements, each of which follows its own purpose.

Natural disasters, which often cause great suffering to human beings are not to be blamed on a flawed genius or a vengeful God. It is true that these discordant notes of a yet unfinished creation disturb humans and make them suffer. However, Irenaeus refuses to see the inequalities of the world as reasons to be surprised or scandalized. Creation is neither perverse nor tragic for those who are receptive to the overall melody of the cosmos, and those who trust the Divine Artist – the very Artist who will mold the human body from the world he created. Irenaeus admits that we do not always understand why God lets us suffer in this world. It is almost as if He had nothing to do with it; the world has its own coherence in which God has no part to play. The important thing is that we know that God will not abandon us, just as the artist who loves his handiwork protects it as much as possible from any impending damage.

Irenaeus does not expect human beings to give up their intellect when confronted with a world working according to its own laws as if there were no room for human intelligence and freedom. For him, it is clear that they must exercise their lordship over the world since it was created for them.

At the same time, they must keep the faith, thankful that they can see the ultimate meaning of the world in its creator. In this respect, Irenaeus is closer to Semitic thinking than to Greek. There was no room in his thinking for the Greek concept of the universe, which totally excluded human responsibility. Although humans cannot fully fathom the mystery of creation, they must not believe the world, including themselves, to be abandoned to pure luck, to blind determinism. For Irenaeus, the *how* and the *why* of the cosmos will be gradually revealed to them in their progress towards God, *"Not one of the things which have been, or are, or shall be made, escapes the knowledge of God, but that through His providence every one of them has obtained its nature, and rank, and number, and special quantity, and that nothing whatever either has been or is produced in vain or accidentally, but on the contrary with exceeding suitability and deep harmony and sublime art."* (A.H. Bk II, 26: 3)

Irenaeus is so convinced of the presence of God in the world, of the dignity of the world as a work worthy of its Creator, that he sees the whole of creation under the sign of the Cross. From the start, the Author of the world stamped his work with his own mark. *"For the Creator of the world is truly the Word of God: and this is our Lord, who in the last times was made man, existing in this world, and who in an invisible manner contains all things created, and is inscribed in the shape of a cross [or inherent] in the entire creation…" (A.H. Bk V, 18: 3)* [10]

The beginning of humanity's vocation and of its salvation coincides with the beginning of the cosmos which, in an invisible way, already bears the mark of the One who will one day be revealed in the flesh. Hence, God is not absent from the world. On the contrary, it is in Him that the sometimes conflicting dimensions of the cosmos find their resolution and reconciliation. The height, length, and breadth of the world meet in the world's harmonizing principle which is the Cross. It is interesting to note that Irenaeus refers to the Eucharist, the greatest sign of communion between humanity and the created world, in the same context as that of the cosmic cross. For Irenaeus such a parallel is quite coherent. The Eucharist, the greatest gift of creation, makes human beings in the image of God because of the fact that wheat and grapes already start the process of transformation, the growth which God seeks for them.

In an extraordinarily rich synthesis, Irenaeus shows the true logic of creation, *"And as we are His members, we are also nourished by means of the creation…He has acknowledged the cup (which is a*

---

10   "…inscribed in the shape of a cross [or inherent] in the entire creation…" In order to match the French translation from the Greek, our translation takes into account the words "inscribed in the shape of a cross" by adding them to the English translation from the Greek by Alexander Roberts and William Rambaut. See translators' note at the end of the book, page 201.

part of the creation) as His own blood, from which He bedews our blood; and the bread (also a part of the creation) He has established as His own body, from which He gives increase to our bodies." (A.H. Bk V, 2: 2)

Just as God takes human flesh from the clay of the earth, so that it might become the workplace of creation, so the Eucharist, God's true praise, is taken from the earth to nourish human flesh until the incorruptibility of eternal life. Human flesh is itself the field in which God sows life. And, in order to highlight this point, Irenaeus says that not only is the cosmos marked by the sign of its Creator, but so is the field of this world. For Christ is *"the treasure which was hid in the field", that is, in this world, for "the field is the world." (A.H. Bk IV, 26: 1)*

Creation cannot be bad since the Word itself is hidden there. Thus, it is perfectly just and reasonable for our bodies to take part in the Eucharist. The latter is composed of two things, the earthly and the celestial. It thus nourishes the human being who is the place where these things meet in the flesh and the spirit. To sum up, the fundamental part played by creation aims at overcoming the limits of life in the resurrection, which is not considered as a process alien to the created world and to today's life. The 'earnest,' the beginning of incorruptibility, is already sown in our mortal bodies by the Eucharist. The Eucharist, the pre-eminent gift of creation, prepares our bodies to assume their full dimension in the image of God.

In order to understand the teaching of Irenaeus about the connection between God and this created world, one may summarize it in six points:

• Creation is not derived from corruption; it is not a place of exile.

- A harmonious cosmos comes from the Wisdom of the Father Almighty. In other words, it is the work of His own Hands, the Spirit and the Word.

- The world is unfinished but good; it is growing because it has been created – and the Creator Himself is involved in its growth.

- The harmony of the world rules out neither suffering nor human freedom. The symphony of the world does not rule out 'dissonances,' because it is not yet a finished work. Its ultimate harmony relies on its Artist-Creator.

- The Word is never absent from the world; it is the hidden treasure in the field of this world; His Cross is present throughout the universe.

- The principle of growth and transformation of the creation is the Eucharist. Taken from the earth in order to become the gift of creation, it saves our flesh from death by preparing it for incorruptibility, the crowning of the creative process.

The Image of God is Inscribed In Human Flesh

What we have just learned about creation, about the meaning of the created world, is to be seen with humanity. Irenaeus' teaching on the mission of human beings in this world takes up the same themes of growth, of the goodness of the created world and of the intimate presence of the Creator in His creation. He goes even further, for the vocation of human beings is not only about transforming their own selves but also about going beyond themselves. In Genesis, not only does God's creative word make human beings but It also gives them their vocation. "Let us make human beings in our image, to be like us." (Genesis 1:26). [11]

Of all creation, only human beings received the vocation to surpass their primeval state.[12] All other species were created 'perfect' in the sense that they were to remain forever what they were when they were created. Their purpose did not require any modification from their original state. But, with human beings things are different. The call for being in the image and likeness means that, from the start, humanity was defined in terms of a vocation. Humans must become what they really are, the image of God. At the moment of their creation they were guided towards God because of their likeness to their Creator. Thus Irenaeus managed to say something fundamental because of the fact that humans walk towards God as humans, they are on God's side because they are human beings.

Conversely, human beings will achieve perfect likeness to their creator when they have fully attained their stature as humans. This is how Irenaeus replied to Gnostic pessimism which regarded the body as a threat to the spiritual being. Irenaeus replied that what was an essential component of the human vocation should not be despised. Indeed, the body is so much a part of the vocation of a human being that it is called upon to be part of the glory of God. The human in its entirety will attain the glory of God. As Irenaeus says, "*...in order that man, having embraced the Spirit of God, might pass*

---

11 Genesis 1:26 New Living Translation (NLT) "Let us make human beings in our image, to be like us."

Genesis 1:26 New International Version (NIV) "Let us make mankind in our image, in our likeness."

Genesis 1:26 King James Version (KJV) "Let us make man in our image, after our likeness."

12 It still remains valid from the viewpoint of the evolutionary science initiated in the 19th century. Regardless of their forebears, a fish, a frog, a monkey have no vocation to surpass their animal state.

into the glory of the Father." (A.H. Bk IV, 20: 4) Never will the Spirit let go of what is His!

This stress on the fact that the human in its entirety was created to take part in the glory of God is important in appreciating Irenaeus' anthropology. What is a human being according to Irenaeus? When he speaks of the soul, like all the thinkers of his time, he is not thinking of something separate from the body. It would have been unthinkable for Irenaeus to speak of an intelligent, insubstantial, and independently existing part of a human being, which is separate from the body. An intelligence without a body is not a human being. Humans who walk towards God do so as incarnate spirits. Their corporeality is the very place of their greatness, because they are called upon to be like the Son made flesh. We shall see further on, how this idea is not in contradiction with life as it is experienced in illness, deformations, mutilations, etc.

We can see an example of the positive aspect of the human corporeal state in what is said by Irenaeus about marriage. He debunked the Gnostic myth describing creation as the result of sexual intercourse between a woman and a bad creator or demiurge. The Gnostic error consisted in annihilating God's great design creating humanity as male and female. They went even further, since by condemning marriage and procreation they implicitly criticized God himself for creating humans as sexual beings, *"(they) preached against marriage, thus setting aside the original creation of God, and indirectly blaming Him who made the male and female for the propagation of the human race." (A.H. Bk I, 28: 1)*

The human – body, breath and spirit – living by the spirit

Mentioning the duality, body-soul, introduces us to a very interesting and important topic to understand the part played by the Spirit in relation to us. It must be noticed here how Irenaeus' thinking draws its inspiration not from the Greek philosophy of his time but from the Bible. The French word *âme* (*soul* in English) is the translation of the biblical term *nephesh*, even if it is impossible to put an equal sign between them. In Semitic thought *nephesh* is neither a pre-existing entity nor is it linked with the divine. It belongs to the created world. It is not viewed as a substantial essence separate from the body. *Nephesh*, or the soul of the human, is linked to the breath that the first human being took in through his nostrils. It is the power that established a 'living soul'.

In other words, *nephesh* is not the body, but it is the body in so far as the latter is alive. We can say that *nephesh* expresses the way for a human being to be human. Everything a human being experiences, everything that is part of his or her worldly existence is due to the fact that he or she is a 'living soul' or *nephesh*. What about death then? When *nephesh* withdraws, the person itself is forced to go 'elsewhere.' It dies because the usual means to express itself is no longer available. (There is no word in Hebrew for *corpse*, nothing expresses the idea of a 'dead human,' it is self-contradictory.)

Hebrew also uses another word when referring to humans: *rûah*. In French we say 'esprit' (*spirit* in English). *Rûah* is 'God's breath,' the very breath that gives life to the human. It is *rûah* that makes the human a *nephesh* or living soul. *Rûah*, or the spirit, comes from God. It is within the human without coming from it. In other words, *rûah*, or the spirit within us, is that which makes us capable of receiving the Spirit of God.

This way of speaking is very important when it comes to the question of the perfection of the human. If Irenaeus uses the word *spirit* to refer to the divine in the human as well as to speak of a reality of his own, what can be said about the perfection of the human imbued with the Spirit? In order to reply to this question, we can look at a text in which Irenaeus describes the perfect human being in terms of body, soul, and spirit, *"for the perfect man consists in the commingling and the union of the soul receiving the spirit of the Father and the admixture of that fleshly nature which was molded after the image of God." (A.H. Bk V, 6: 1)*

For the publishers of *Sources chrétiennes*, it is clear that the spirit that Irenaeus is speaking about here is the Divine Spirit. The perfect human being is thus one who has got the Divine Spirit. Does this mean that the Divine Spirit is additional to a human being?

Were this the case, a human would essentially be body and soul, nothing else. The third component, 'the Spirit' would be extrinsic, a 'supernatural' component, unnecessary for natural perfection. How does Irenaeus present things? He writes about the human as such, *"...we are [composed of] a body taken from the earth, and a soul receiving spirit from God." (A.H. Bk III, 22: 1)*

Other texts help us understand the meaning of this assertion so *"the soul herself is not life, but partakes in that life bestowed upon her by God". (A.H. Bk II, 34: 4)* The human soul has no life of its own but exists only by means of a divine force that Irenaeus calls either 'breath of life' or 'Spirit,' that is to say *rûah* of the Bible. It is God's breath which is therefore the origin of human breath, *nephesh*. Without this divine force, a human being is not alive. And, this is true regardless of any question about perfection or sanctity. For Irenaeus, as for the Bible, the life that animates body and soul comes from God. It is always a gift. As a result even the sinner is alive thanks to the gift of God, thanks to *rûah* animating *nephesh!* How then can one distinguish the divine force which animates human beings (the 'breath of life') from the vivifying Spirit which makes them perfect? This is a difficult point which created many problems for Irenaeus' commentators. Whatever the answer, one must stress that for Irenaeus the source of all human animation is divine. It is not about two lives that differ in kind, but about one human being, alive and different depending on the will to live according to the Spirit or not.

The life of God in humans

In saying this, I think that we now know enough to get to the heart of Irenaeus' thinking about the Spirit; the Spirit present in humans right from the beginning – without which they would not even be human. A human being living in the divine Spirit is none other than a human living by the breath of God. It is necessary to go back to the dynamic idea of growth in order to resolve the difficulty.

Right from the beginning, human beings are unfinished, that is to say, they are called upon to grow and to be fulfilled according to the spirit which is already in them, though in an imperfect manner. What distinguishes humans who are called 'spiritual' from those called 'natural' is neither two different levels of existence nor two different principles of life, but it is the way in which they cope with their vocation by the use of their freedom. The Divine Spirit is with all humans right from the beginning for It alone is the source of all life. A human as a whole – and all humans – feel the need to become more and more alive in the Spirit. Starting from a frail initial state, a human as a whole is to progress slowly but surely towards life in all its fullness.

If one reads Irenaeus in the light of the principle that he himself insisted upon, i.e. *growth*, the words he used become easier to understand: *nature, soul, substance, body etc.* They retrieve the original meanings they have in the Bible. The word substance is precisely such an example. When Irenaeus says, *"My soul also shall live to Him, just as if its substance were immortal." (A.H. Bk V, 7: 1)*, one has no need to go further than the Bible to understand what he means. The Greek word used here (*huparxousis* and not *ousia*) is dynamic. One can well see how this word resonates when looking at the cognate verb (*huparxo*). In Greek, this verb simply means 'I am,' 'I exist.' It refers to the living reality of a being, to what it is, as a result of what happens to it in life. Its 'substance,' in this case, is not the stable essence of the Greek philosophy (*ousia*) but the non-speculative reality of the Bible, 'what I am,' that is to say, the reality of my being (or my substance), which will not die because it received the breath of God from the start. Thanks to the divine breath, the human is thrown into the world as one who is not destined for annihilation. Since their creation, humans have been entirely established on the way to incorruptibility. Such is the normal condition of humanity. Irenaeus' anthropology goes as far as that. One must really understand this point in order to grasp the theological vision of human beings in Irenaeus.

We have already seen some implications of the image of the *Hands of God* for Irenaeus' thinking. This very image permits him to go even further to clarify the idea that human beings were created in the image and the likeness of God.

"But man He formed with His own hands, taking from the earth that which was purest and finest, and mingling in measure His own power with the earth. For He traced His own form on the formation, that that which should 'be seen should be of divine form: for the image of God was man formed and set on the earth'." (Dem.11)

When one reads this passage for the first time, one wonders whether he or she understands it properly. God sealed in the human flesh the mark of His own image! How does one understand such an unexpected teaching, such an idea which seems to run counter to all evidence and even to common sense? (An idea which Saint Augustine was unable to accept two hundred years later!) What makes the idea of God's stamp in the human flesh somewhat difficult to understand is the lack of explanation in Irenaeus. He is more interested in the *why* than in the *how* of this idea, which he thinks he can find in Genesis. God shaped the 'modeling clay' of human beings in His own image so that it might bear the gift of incorruptibility deriving from the fact that flesh partakes of the Spirit. The creation of human beings in the image of God is thus a true token of His glorious purpose. This is what A. Orbe says, "The mystery lies in the fact that human beings alone were fashioned in the image of God….The Creator delights in stamping the origin of humans with an outstanding mark of salvation for which they are destined." [13]

What is this 'image of God' in the flesh of a human being? After studying a fair number of texts, it seems to me, that this 'mark' of God is no more than His life in us, the life of God which makes the whole human being live with a view to incorruptibility. This conclusion is reinforced by the idea that, in Irenaeus as in Saint Paul, whom he quotes in this context, the notion of image is not a static one, is not unchangeable. Paul says that Christ has not jealously kept 'the form of God' (see Ph 2: 6-7 "Who, being in very nature God…he made himself nothing by taking the very nature of a servant, being made in human likeness.)

Here, 'image' means something in the process of becoming and of fulfilling itself – a manifestation getting clearer and clearer, radiant with the presence that it evokes. Human beings, bearing in

---

13 A. Orbe, *Antropologia de San Irenero*, Madrid, La Editoria Catolica, coll. "Biblioteca de autores cristianos," 1969, p. 40.

their flesh the image of the Uncreated, are called upon to fully actualize the life of God within them. Now the two Hands of the Father, the Word and the Spirit, ensure the ever-continuing growth of this clay modeled in the image of God. This leads us to the key question, if the Spirit is the source of human life, how does It become the person's true life? How can a human created in the image of God become the truly, fully living image of God? I think that the answer to these questions is to be found where Irenaeus himself found the basis of his theology, that is to say, in the Bible.

In Genesis, as in all of the Old Testament, the phrase 'created in the image of God' does not refer to a moral relationship between the human and the divine. The Jewish Bible does not refer to an 'image' which would be 'lost' because of sin. Similarly, nowhere does Irenaeus say that Adam or his descendants have ceased to be in the image of God after sin. Thus, the phrase 'human beings, created in the image of God,' highlights the specificity of human nature compared with all other creatures. Humans have always been the image of God. But, Irenaeus thinks that this image is very frail at the start. Newly-created human beings are still far from perfection and the incorruptibility for which they are ultimately destined. Hence, at the beginning, they were 'an image of God' still unfinished; they were in their infancy, as Irenaeus put it.

Their vocation to grow as an image of God coincided with their creation. For this reason, as we have already seen, the source of life, the Spirit, is not an additional component. Right from the start, a human being is a living soul thanks to the Spirit. But, humans need to be worked on from within by the Spirit so that they may attain their true dignity as an image of God. To go back to the idea that the image of God in their flesh is no more than life, it can now be said that the perfecting of this image, its fulfillment, is the work of the Spirit. The human who obeys God lives fully 'the communion in Spirit.' In other words, according to Irenaeus, the 'perfect' human and the 'imperfect' human are not two different levels of reality. They are two ways of describing live situations, moments when the openness to, or the rejection of the Spirit reveal human beings as fully alive or not.

Indeed, it can be said that Irenaeus' entire theology revolves around the themes of life and growth in order to make the whole of humankind incorruptible, even the flesh which bears the mark of the divine. It is therefore the *end* and not the *beginning* which determines the 'raison d'être' of our lives. The perfection of human beings, their likeness to God, is kept for the end.

Becoming Human Is A Process of Growth

There is one final question to be addressed before dealing with the second article of the *Apostles' Creed*, namely that of Adam and Eve. [14] We are not about to go back over the first chapters of Genesis in detail. This is not Irenaeus' way nor will it be ours. What is interesting to note is to see how Irenaeus' interpretation of the first couple picks up the same themes that we have already seen. The notion of created life implies that of growth, the notion of the image cannot be viewed separately from that of the vocation or the ability of humans to respond freely to God's call. All these ideas can be summed up in a single assertion, by freedom, *a human is set in history as a being in the process of becoming*. Irenaeus' teaching about Adam allows us to see closely all the implications of this assertion.

---

14 Is it still worth mentioning that the stories in Genesis are concerned with the why and not the how of creation? Adam and Eve are not to be taken as historical people but as representatives of the beginning of humanity. (Editor's note.)

I have said that the image of God in humanity is frail at the beginning. When newly born one's hold on life is precarious. This reality is behind much of Irenaeus' teaching about Adam. Let us bear in mind the teaching about the child who will one day be ruler. This is quite in keeping with Irenaeus' thinking because he presents Adam and Eve as children: "But man was a child, not yet having his understanding perfected; wherefore also he was easily led astray by the deceiver." (Dem. 12)

"But inasmuch as they are not uncreated, for this very reason do they [Adam and Eve] come short of the perfect. Because, as these things are of later date, so are they infantile; so are they unaccustomed to, and unexercised in, perfect discipline." (A.H.Bk IV, 38: 1)

I think that it would be a mistake to want to know whether Irenaeus meant that the first couple was really created in the state of infancy. What is important here is the fact that a human is a being in the process of becoming – but not just any being. The becoming to which he or she is called is the task of the *Hands of God*, the Word, and the Spirit. They watch over, so to speak, the beginnings of human life by getting themselves involved in fulfilling the task of establishing it and making it 'perfect.' Because the human is newly created, life in him or her is not very hardy. It lacks the energy required to stand up to the destructive forces which seek to destroy it.

Further on, in the context of *redemption*, we shall see the implications of this approach for what is referred to as 'Adam's sin' or 'original sin.' But, for the moment, let us note that, in Irenaeus' eyes, this sin of Adam did not entail all the dreadful consequences for humanity elaborated in a later tradition. For Irenaeus, the image of Adam as a child has profound implications in the understanding of the relationship between God and human beings. A mortal and newly created nature is frail. This is why it cannot immediately bear the immense load of the glory that God keeps in store for it. Time is needed before we reach the state when we can bear, even welcome, this gift. Irenaeus would say that our life should be established and bound together by the work of the Word and the Spirit within us.

"He who made, and formed, and breathed in them the breath of life, and nourishes us by means of the Creation, establishing all things by His Word, and binding them together by His Wisdom [the Son and the Spirit], this is He who is the only true God." (A.H. Bk III, 24: 2)

Of course, this way of speaking implies that life – all life and all forms of life – come from God. This is exactly what the biblical authors believed, particularly Saint Paul for whom life was not intrinsic to created beings. In whatever way it manifests itself, life always comes from somewhere else. It is never the product of human will. In this respect we move, without a break, from the biological and physical level of life to the psychic and spiritual level; life, the work of God, is always *one*.

It is one and the same life during which human beings live in time and make their way towards incorruptibility. The life that God makes humans live is always *one* in spite of its varied forms. If one lives life badly, one lives inhumanely. Irenaeus goes even further, saying that whoever lives life badly is already dead in spite of appearances, *"The flesh, therefore, when destitute of the Spirit of God, is dead, not having life, and cannot possess the kingdom of God... But where the Spirit of the Father is, there is a living man."* (A.H. Bk V, 9: 3)

It seems to me that one cannot be more explicit. It is not about two different states, but about one and the same life lived differently. It was true for Adam, and it is true for us. The greater the presence of the Spirit, the more alive we are. On all levels – biological, psychic and spiritual – our growth is always a gift, always the work of the Spirit. And, the Adam-child image is probably the best illustration of this principle. In this, one can see very clearly the idea that life in human beings is a portent of what they have not yet been and of what they can become, thanks to the Spirit already in them. So, they are destined to reach plenitude and the perfection of the image after which they were created. The plenitude of their lives in the Spirit reveals the image that humans are in all their truth.

One can object here that this theology puts all responsibility on God's side. We cannot see very clearly the part played by human freedom in this case. In order to refute this objection, one must go back to the idea of the image. Who is the perfect image of the Father? Saint Paul tells us about it, "The Son is the image of the invisible God, the firstborn over all creation." (Col 1: 15) Now Irenaeus says, God made human beings in his image, "the image of God is the Son, after whose image man was made." (Dem. 22) Humans are in the image of the perfect Image of God, that is to say the Son. This means that, according to the formal order, according to the order of principles, Incarnation takes place *before* the fashioning of Adam and all humanity. All, including the first human being, are created after the image of the Son, the perfect image of God:

"For in times long past, it was said that man was created after the image of God, but it was not (actually) shown; for the Word was as yet invisible, after whose image man was created: wherefore also he did easily lose the similitude. When, however, the Word of God became flesh, He confirmed both these: for He both showed forth the image truly..." (A.H. Bk V, 16: 2)

Everything is coherent in Irenaeus' vision. One cannot isolate one aspect without distorting the rest, without bringing in an error. Creation and Incarnation are here presented as inextricably linked. The creative Word, invisible in times gone by, makes Himself visible so that human beings may see the image after which they were fashioned. By becoming Himself human, the Word reveals that His own life is that by which humans live, the life of Him whom they look like.

How does this way of seeing things leave room for freedom? For Irenaeus, the true accomplishment of human beings will take place by letting go the old self in order to fully and freely embrace the Word after which they were fashioned. Y*et, paradoxically, this move towards the Author of their lives is simultaneously the greatest act of fidelity of human beings towards themselves.* That is true because they were not made in the image of God as a sort of 'duplicate.' They are 'informed,' at every level of their being, of what makes them in the likeness of God. To sum up, they are not a 'copy' of the divine; *they are the image of God*, which is something totally different.

Let us recall that in Irenaeus, a dynamic process is always at work. This is why the Adam-child image helps us to understand this. The unfinished state at the beginning means that the limits of the fashioning were not fixed in advance. Adam can aspire to be in the likeness of the Word because he received incompletely the divine form in his flesh. And yet, it is an aspiration which preserves his autonomy. Humans do not relinquish their own selves by letting themselves join in the Glory of God. In fact, Irenaeus sees in the original frailty in which human beings were created the very warranty for their autonomy and freedom. Called upon to be in the image of the Word, a human being is only free in so far as he or she is able to realize and assert what he or she is. This implies in humans the capacity to say 'yes,' and to say yes freely with no strings attached. To sum up, human freedom in Irenaeus lies in the ability to follow freely and without constraint the One after whom human beings were fashioned. ■

CHAPTER III

I Believe in Jesus Christ His Only Son, Our Lord, Who Was Conceived by the Holy Spirit, Born of the Virgin Mary

It is now clear that Irenaeus' teaching is to be seen as a whole. He never refers to a specific aspect of faith without pointing out where it fits in to the overall message. We have just been dealing with Creation as a process of growth towards the Glory of God, born of a promise sown into our frail beginnings. Moving on to the question of the Incarnation is not, for Irenaeus, moving on to a second chapter in the story of salvation while leaving the first behind; rather, it is about taking up the same story of Creation from the viewpoint of its own internal logic. The advent of the Son among us is in keeping with the Creation of human beings in the image of God.

Incarnation Fits the Logic of Creation

For Irenaeus, it was as normal as can be that the Word that presided over the creation of human beings should Himself come to His own things – this very world – to reveal the full meaning of His creation to humans. In other words, Incarnation is part of the original design. It is not an afterthought as if it were just a way of righting the wrong committed by sinners. To say that the Incarnation was a response to sin, in order to make adjustments or to rectify God's design thwarted by human wickedness would mean that sin comes first.

This would also mean that sin could, as it were, determine God's behavior! Admittedly, Irenaeus does not state this explicitly, and this for a very simple reason. The idea of a God who would have changed His mind, or who would have decided to make up for sin by sending His Son, could not be part of a *theology of growth*. On the contrary, right from the creation of human beings, the Incarnation is seen as a necessity. This is implicit in Irenaeus' commentary on the story of the man born blind in John 9:1-41. *"Wherefore also the Lord spat on the ground and made clay, and smeared it upon the eyes, pointing out the original fashioning (of man)."* (A.H. Bk V, 15: 2)

If we pay attention to the meaning of the words in the quotation, something quite surprising becomes clear: the Lord who restores sight to the man born blind is the Word, the craftsman, the 'artificer,' He who presided over Creation. Now, the hand of the Lord, the historic Christ, repeats the same act of creation that was in the beginning. Without falling into a simplistic and linear chronology, which was not Irenaeus' aim, we can say here that, as soon as they were created, human beings turned towards God and were eager to *see* Him.

Seeing God is inscribed in their flesh as a promise. By enabling the man born blind to *see*, the Son indicates that the initial design to *see* God one day remains intact in spite of sin. The Incarnation is there not only to say that God stands by His creation, but also to hasten and facilitate its fulfillment.

Were we to follow Irenaeus' reasoning to its logical conclusion, we would have to say that the Incarnation was not first and foremost the means chosen by God to make up for the disobedience of Adam and his descendants. This idea is not specified in Irenaeus' text, but it is significant that in the context of the man born blind, he does not evoke a cure (strictly speaking) but the actualization of a potential, according to the words of Jesus, "Neither has this man sinned, nor his parents: but that the works of God should be made manifest in him." (Jn 9: 3)

The hand of Jesus opens the eyes of the man born blind so that he might know and recognize the Creative Hand of the Word already at work at the dawn of Creation. Seen from this perspective, the Incarnation is part of the logic of Creation by a God who not only stands by the work He started, but who also comes closer and closer to it. In fact, there comes a time when He openly manifests Himself, when He becomes human so that human beings might become what He is.

This seems to me to be the core of Irenaeus' thinking about the Incarnation. Of course, Irenaeus also speaks of the liberation from sin carried out by the Incarnate Son, but there again, sin cannot be the main cause for His Advent. In the preface to Book V, Irenaeus delivers the core of his belief as regards to the why of the Incarnation. He asks his reader to follow *"the only true and steadfast Teacher, the Word of God, our Lord Jesus Christ, who did, through His transcendent love, become what we are, that He might bring us to be even what He is Himself."* (A.H. Bk V, preface)

Why then the Incarnation? It is to ensure the fulfillment of the work of love started with the creation of human beings. In a negative sense, the liberation from sin is part of this fulfillment. In a positive sense, all humans, sinners or not, need to know the

Hand by which they were fashioned so that their growth might be accomplished through their likeness to God. By applying the theme of growth to this need to know the Artist who fashioned human beings, Irenaeus puts forward an unusual teaching about the Incarnation. Yet it is solid and theologically well-grounded. This is what we are going to see in more detail.

God Became Human So That Human Beings Might Become "Fully Alive"

Nothing is more obvious for Irenaeus: human beings need God. They need God in order to become what they are designed to be. But, this vocation can only be fulfilled where they naturally stand – *in this world.* Their need for God is thus inseparable from their worldly condition. It is *in this world,* and not elsewhere, that humans are to meet their God. If Irenaeus insists on this point, it is because he does not want the Christians to follow the Gnostics and miss their meeting with God. To flee from this world, as the Gnostics advocate, is to run the risk of passing by the Lord without recognizing Him. It also means to deny the place, the spot, which God has chosen for human beings.

These will enjoy the fruit of incorruptibility only by addressing the affairs of this world. In Irenaeus, this intimate link between their yearning and the worldly dwelling in which they fulfill their vocation is inseparable from the Incarnation. It is by staying in *this world* that they can meet their Lord. It is in *this world* that the links between human beings and the Incarnate Word are woven. Indeed, it is because human beings need to touch, to hear, and to see the visible things with their own bodies that the Incarnation can be an event true to human nature. It is true to a nature that grows more quickly when in the presence of its model, "We could not in any other way participate in incorruption, save by His coming among us. For so long as incorruption was invisible and unrevealed, it helped us not at all. Therefore, it became visible, that in all respects we might participate in the reception of incorruption." (Dem. 31)

According to this logic, it can be said that the Son has come into this world to give credibility to the vocation of human beings. When seeing their Lord filled with the perfection of the heritage they were awaiting, they could better live up to such hope. By making Himself visible, the Divine Artist asserts their worth and their vocation. *"And then, again, this Word was manifested when the Word of God was made man, assimilating Himself to man, and man to Himself, so that by means of his resemblance to the Son, man might become precious to the Father."* (A.H. Bk V, 16: 2)

Thus, it seems that the Incarnation was bound to happen in any case. It was necessary for humans to be aware of their vocation so that they should never again question why they had been created. Clearly, it is something to be wished for. But, given human nature, this is not obvious for one simple reason: learning needs time. Understanding requires human beings to have a program in which time, patience, and teaching skills play a very important part. It is within this learning context that Irenaeus places the coming of the Lord in this world in terms of the Incarnation. Although the Word manifested Himself through various epiphanies or occasional events (such as dreams, visions and prophetic utterances), He reveals himself in a way better suited to the human condition at the optimal time in history. The theme of *accustomization* is quite appropriate when dealing with Incarnation as a way of teaching.

Let us recall what John says in his first epistle, "What was from the beginning, what we have heard, what we have seen with our eyes, what we looked upon and touched with our hands concerns the Word of life." (1 Jn 1: 1) It can be said without exaggeration that Irenaeus' entire work is nothing other than an extended commentary on this verse. The Son came to reveal the *true* Gnosis, the *true knowledge* of the Father (which the Gnostics refused). Now, in this scheme, the part played by Spirit is a major one, for this work of revelation – knowledge of the truth – is essentially that of the Spirit who reveals the Father in the Son. It is a task of education! *"The Spirit of God furnishes us with a knowledge of the truth, and has set forth the dispensations of the Father and the Son, in virtue of which He dwells with every generation of men."* (A.H. Bk IV, 33: 7)

The work of our true teacher, the Spirit (Divine Wisdom), reveals the true Gnosis which is the knowledge of the Father and the Son. This goes very far, for the revealing work of the Spirit also concerns the Incarnate Son Himself. Not only does the Spirit teach us who the Son is, but also teaches the Son what it is to be a human being! The Spirit accustoms the Son to the company of humans so that His stay among us might be the opportunity for a true transformation of the relationship between God and human beings. By descending onto the Son during His baptism, the Spirit managed a true 'feat' so to speak, as the event was precious not only for humans but also for God. On the one hand, the Spirit has accustomed the Son to dwell in the human race, as He has done himself from the beginning and, on the other hand, He opens a new chapter in the relationship between the humans and God. By visibly accompanying the Son, human beings are renewed by the knowledge of God, which transforms *them*, brings *them* really close to God.

"Wherefore He did also descend upon the Son of God, made the Son of man, becoming accustomed in fellowship with Him to dwell in the human race, to rest with human beings, and to dwell in the workmanship of God, working the will of the Father in them, and re-

newing them from their old habits into the newness of Christ." (A.H. Bk III, 17: 1)

In these words, we can hear an echo of Saint Paul about the New self. For example, in Ephesians 4:22, about putting off the old self and the spiritual transformation of intelligence in putting on the new self, and in Colossians 3:10 about the knowledge which gives permanent access to a renewed being in the image of its creator.

This is to be noted because in Paul the context is obviously moral. In both cases (Ephesians and Colossians) Paul speaks of the necessity for the sinner to be converted "(his self) being corrupted by its deceitful desires…" What about Irenaeus? He does not mention it in spite of his reference to Paul. While speaking of the new self transformed by the Spirit through the Son, he avoids the moral stance in this requirement and does not moralize. What stands out, in the way Irenaeus reads Paul, is the image of humans in need of such great enlightenment that they no longer need to fumble in seeking the way as they used to do in the past, when the Word was still invisible. Thanks to the new knowledge that the Incarnation grants them as to their true nature, human beings can enter a new stage in their relationship with God, and get a second wind to resume their project with renewed impetus.

Now they *know* clearly what they are because they *see* Him after whom they were created. In other words, now they know with certainty whom they resemble. The idea is so important in Irenaeus that if all this were untrue, if human beings were not in the image of God, one would have to come to the conclusion that either Christ has not come or that He came in vain. Fortunately, the Spirit is there to avoid such an eventuality since He is the one who makes humans aware that they were made in the image of God. If they did not know this truth, true right from the beginning, it was not because they were forsaken by God, but because they were blind. They did not know that they were precious in the eyes of God, hence their disease and misery. Irenaeus' interpretation of the parable of the man born blind runs along these lines. Physical blindness is for him linked with ignorance, not with sin. His intelligence lacked the enlightenment of the Spirit. When the Son opens his eyes, the man born blind sees the creative Hand of the Son. He becomes a seer capable of following his path, the only one that is really his, i.e. the Son. *"I am the Way and the Truth and the Life." (Jn 14:6 and A.H. Bk IV, 7: 3)*

What conclusion must we come to? That the Incarnation fully actualizes the image of God in the flesh: for human beings to be in the likeness of God, God must be in the likeness of humankind. This is the way in which God is true to His creation.

God's steadfast love tirelessly tracks humankind to the point of taking on the features of His creation located in space and time. God's design for humans did not come into being in the unfathomable depths of the Divine Being but in history. And, it has a human face, Jesus Christ. From this viewpoint, it is not a matter of talking about God first and then about humans. Conversely, Irenaeus does not imagine that human beings can be truly viewed independently from God. Nothing can be said about humans without mentioning their relationship with God, and conversely!

For Irenaeus, to reflect on humanity is to reflect on God. Humanity is where God is, just as God is where humanity is. This is why the Incarnation cannot be limited to a single event in history. Because it has created such links between humans and God, it is still at work in humankind as a pledge for its fulfillment. It recapitulates all human beings, from Adam to the last member of the human race. It seems to me essential to bear this idea in mind in order to understand properly the second part of the article of the *Apostles' Creed* with which we are now dealing, "Our Lord [...] was conceived by the Holy Spirit, born of the Virgin Mary..."

The Virgin Birth, Warranty of Our Hope

Let us start with a relevant quote, "*...therefore, the Lord Himself, who is Emmanuel from the Virgin is the sign of our salvation, since it was the Lord Himself who saved them, because they could not be saved by their own instrumentality...*" (*A.H. Bk III, 20: 3*)

These few lines show that what Irenaeus says about Christ, born of the Virgin Mary, is a teaching about the identity of Christ and the salvation of humanity.[15] Irenaeus' reference to Isaiah 7:14 is clear, "The young woman will conceive and give birth to a son." But, given the context, it is also clear that Irenaeus' full attention is focused on the finality of the Incarnation and on the reality of God's design achieved through His Son.

It seems to me, that the way he insists on the virgin birth in this design serves to throw light on two aspects of the matter: firstly, the identity of Jesus and secondly, the quality of our hope.

To express the identity of Jesus

For Irenaeus, it is essential to show, to demonstrate, the identity of Christ in order to know the identity of human beings since they are in His image. Thus, the task that Irenaeus undertakes is clear. It is necessary on the one hand to establish the link between the historical Jesus and the Creative Word, and on the other hand to establish the true nature of Jesus' corporeality as well as of our own.

------

15 In other words, the virgin birth is a Christology not a Mariology (in the modern sense).

Irenaeus is careful to keep separate the distinct levels of the history of salvation, especially concerning the presence of the Creative Word with humankind before the Incarnation and the presence of the Incarnate Word in history. For instance, *he never uses the names Jesus or Christ when speaking about the Creative Word.* At the same time, he refers to the Son as the Word, presiding over the construction of the world, as the one who came among us. There again, the Gnostic teachings led Irenaeus to insist on the unity of the work of salvation accomplished by the unity of the Word. For instance, we do not usually think of the Word as being present with Abraham or Moses. But, in Irenaeus' eyes, this teaching was necessary because of the way believers were attracted to Marcion, a Christian who had been excommunicated because of the way he rejected the Creator in the Old Testament as opposed to the Good God revealed in the New Testament.

According to Marcion, Christ only came for those concerned by the New Alliance. In opposition to the idea that called into question the unity of the work of God and God Himself, Irenaeus asserts the identity of the Son as a person. He is none other than the Lord who came among us, *"Therefore the Son of the Father declares (Him) from the beginning, inasmuch as He was with the Father from the beginning." (A.H. Bk .IV, 20: 7)*

By identifying the Creative Word with the Incarnate Word, Irenaeus aims at maintaining the continuity of the work of creation: Christ has made visible the creative activity at work from the beginning.

This means once again that there has been no break within God's unique design for humanity, regardless of the mishaps suffered by the latter in the course of their progress towards God. The Incarnation is there to say that the hope that it inspires in us is justified.

But, to say that the coming of the Son into this world is a reason for hope is not enough. It is also essential to explain the way in which the virgin birth is necessary to give coherence to this hope.

Mary, one of us, says "yes"

With Irenaeus the basic idea is that the virgin birth was necessary to maintain firmly the link between Christ's humanity and his divinity, and hence, to ensure the reality of the creative design for us. I have just mentioned the continuity of the Presence of the Word in this world – invisible before the Incarnation, visible afterwards.

This very idea of continuity is evoked to speak of the link between Incarnate Christ and humankind. Yet, Irenaeus sees very clearly the difficulty in the latter assertion that if Christ, entirely born of our human race, is totally imprisoned in the lineage of humans – uninterrupted since Adam – he cannot do anything for himself and his fellow beings. It would be unthinkable for anyone of the human race to emerge on his or her own from this living mass of humans stained by sin. Though it is intact, the image of God in which human beings were made remains too weak to produce their own savior. Humanity has no possibility to overcome the sinful condition in which it is mired. In other words, the person, able to lift the obstacles on our way and to establish us in the likeness of God, cannot be another sinner.

In order to become fully and truly in the likeness of God, humans need someone born of their race but, at the same time, freed from everything that makes their own weakness, their ignorance and their sins. What would be needed, as Irenaeus says, is a 'new birth', a birth due to neither the will of the flesh nor to human will, but rather to the goodwill of the Father. As long as the human race is closed in on itself, it will be unable, on its own, to bring about its own salvation. Unaided, it will be unable to surmount the necessary difference to overcome sin and death.

Like begets like. It is necessary that like should be open to the difference in order to be transformed. This is precisely Irenaeus' guiding principle in what he says about the Incarnation being a 'new birth,' being a pledge or warranty for our own new birth.

The starting point is, as we have just seen, the Father's goodwill. God's entirely free love gives birth to the One who breaks the line of human beings incapable of achieving by themselves the extraordinary project which calls them into being. In order to show how the new birth of Christ, foreseen from the beginning, is a warranty for our new birth, Irenaeus arrives at an extraordinary synthesis between the liturgical tradition and the sacramental dimension of the Eucharist to assert the image of God in the flesh.

Indeed, Irenaeus notices that a group of believers, the Ebionites, do not want to accept the new birth achieved by the Spirit through Mary. Their Eucharist, celebrated with water instead of wine, symbolizes this denial. Their denial of the union of God and humanity is called 'vain' by Irenaus. He writes that the Ebionites...

"...do not choose to understand that the Holy Ghost came upon Mary, and the power of the Most High did overshadow her: wherefore also what was generated is a holy thing, and the Son of the Most High, God the Father of all, who...showed forth a new (kind of) generation; that...so by this new generation we might inherit life. Therefore, do these men reject the commixture of the heavenly wine, and wish it to be water of the world only, not receiving God so as to have union with Him...not considering that as...the Word of the Father and the Spirit of God, having become united with the ancient substance of Adam's formation, rendered man living and perfect... And for this reason in the last times, not by the will of the flesh, nor by the will of man, but

by the good pleasure of the Father, His hands formed a living man, in order that Adam might be created (again) after the image and likeness of God. (A.H. Bk V,1: 3)

Without going into a detailed analysis of this very dense text, let us try to pick up the various strands of Irenaeus' thinking.

1. He reminds the Ebionites that the water of baptism will be of no use unless it is mingled with the divine wine, that is to say, the very substance of the Word who mixed with our humanity.

2. By referring to Adam, Irenaeus sends us back to the beginning of humanity. Yet, we must not be mistaken; Adam is not the true beginning of humanity and neither would the last member of our human race be the last representative of our history. The historical beginning and end are recapitulated (as we shall see further on) by the principle of all things, the Hand of God, which is also the aim of human existence. Consequently, it is not possible to introduce anything new other than the birth of the Son into the course of history.

3. If I am not ready to believe that the Son of God was born of the Virgin Mary, I reduce Christ to the level of an ordinary human being (symbolized by the water of the Ebionites) and my baptism becomes a meaningless rite since it would send me back only to myself, to my humanity, which would not be open to the wine of the divinity of the Son.

4. Similarly, the celebration of the Eucharist with only water is symbolically empty, as it signifies that there is nothing new in the birth of Christ. His flesh, the warranty of the image and likeness inscribed in my own flesh, would be reduced to the flesh of an ordinary human being who would be no more able than I am to lead me into incorruptibility.

It is difficult to think of a more balanced synthesis, taking into account the various components of faith in a coherent way. Everything fits together. Far from being an occurrence alien to our history, the Incarnation is its new and definitive birth, not because it puts an end to the economy of salvation (always at work in the world), but because it makes it visible. It is within this context that the part played by the Virgin Mary is to be understood.

We have just seen that the virgin birth is essentially a Christology for Irenaeus, as it provides the key to Jesus' identity in the sense that it corresponds to the need for a savior who would not be imprisoned in the lineage of human beings only born of the will of the flesh. A virgin birth takes Christ out of this lineage because it is the work of the Spirit of God. But, it also ensures the reality of His humanity. Thanks to Mary, Christ is not 'disguised as a man,' as the Docetics would have him.

A purely spiritual Christ without any real contact with our humanity would not have been able to do anything for us. The salvation offered to humankind would be nothing but a tragic lie since the promise signaled by the Incarnation would not be fulfilled. If it were so for those whose hope is grounded in a promise with no future, hell would have already begun.

But, in fact, there is one of the human race who not only believed but also knew the truth about all of that in her body – Mary, the mother of Jesus.

Of all the Church Fathers, it is undoubtedly Irenaeus who comes first for the place he gives to Mary in the work of salvation. It is clear that, for him, Mary's 'fiat,' her saying, "Yes, let it be to me according to your word!" allowed humankind to break out of the vicious circle of sin, in so far as her consent allowed one of its members to escape the power of evil while remaining fully human. If the basis of our hope is the divine and human reality of the Incarnation, we owe it to the mother of Jesus whose 'yes' made it possible.

But, the teaching of Irenaeus on the virgin birth is not a mere academic hypothesis or scholarly point. He does not seek to know *how* the Incarnation took place on the physical level. All he needs is to stick to what was handed down to him by the Apostolic tradition. What he is interested in is the *why* of the virgin birth through which the Incarnation was achieved.

We have already seen that what is at stake is Jesus' identity. As for humankind, it was about a renewed hope through the fact that this new birth, entirely the work of God's will, was to escape the old legacy of death. Consequently, the rest of humanity was no longer in the grip of death. In this, we have the gist of Irenaeus' teaching on the *why* and raison d'être of the virgin birth.

But, Irenaeus does not stop at that in his thinking about the meaning of this event. He carries on further with the idea that the stages which mark human life (birth, growth, maturation, and old age) all fall under the inexorable law of contingency and that religious tradition has viewed physical decay and death as a sign of moral decline (see for example the book of Job). According to this idea, overcoming corruptibility meant overcoming evil.

It is this idea of 'unbounding' which dominates Irenaeus' thinking about Mary. He draws a parallel between the two women, Eve and Mary. In the former, he sees the one who bound up our fate in death. In the latter, he sees the one who, thanks to her 'fiat,' unbound this fate in favor of life. The image of the knot unbound by Mary has very great symbolic power to refute the fatal nature of existence – provided that we do not attribute to Irenaeus the idea that Mary herself was the mediator of salvation.

It is necessary to see how Mary's 'fiat' fits into Irenaeus' thinking. It is an entirely human 'yes.' By her free consent, Mary, a human, is responsible for the coming of Christ our Savior. Thanks to her, the whole of humanity participates in the fruit of salvation made possible by the 'yes' of one of its members. This is the first important idea to bear in mind.

The second leads us straight to the core of Irenaeus' thinking about Mary. He says that she is responsible for the birth of her Son, but he immediately explains what he means. The one who is truly responsible is God, *"But since an unlooked-for salvation was to be provided for men through the help of God, so also was the unlooked-for birth from a Virgin accomplished; God giving this sign, but man not working it out."* (A.H. Bk III, 21: 6)

Jesus, the 'sign,' was the will of God. As for Mary, she makes the true humanity of the Son possible and, by this, ensures that redemption is the work of a true human being. In other words, in order to say who the Son is, Irenaeus had to talk about the mother.

In fact, Mary's 'fiat' indicates the new situation of human faith before God. If human beings had been somehow 'bound' by Eve's sin, it was because of Eve's disbelief, her refusal to believe in the greatness of the design that God had prepared for her and her kin. Conversely, if human beings happened to be 'unbound' by Mary, it was because of her faith. This is what Irenaeus explicitly says, *"For what the virgin Eve had bound fast through unbelief, this did the Virgin Mary set free through faith."* (A.H. Bk III, 22: 4)

Of course, this does not entail any superiority of virginity over sexual intercourse. There is no room for such a moralistic approach in Irenaeus. First, because of the importance he gives to the flesh bearing the image of God, "Irenaeus, at least his argument has nothing to do with any kind of mystique about virginity." [16] Then, because of the guiding principle behind his teaching here, the virgin birth on the symbolic level heralds a new order of fecundity and growth in the process of becoming within the limits of human finiteness. Mary's 'fiat,' confronted by the impossible, made possible the breaking free from the limits of a world turned hard and impenetrable because of sin and death.

From these remarks, one can come to the conclusion that Irenaeus addresses the question of the virgin birth only for Christological reasons. Far from being a way of protecting Christ from any 'contamination' by the ordinary way of human procreation, it means that our humanity is capable of going beyond, of opening itself up to an *Other* who is not afraid of our finiteness. In one of the most beautiful quotations from Irenaeus, we can reach the epitome of his thought as to the necessity of the Incarnation, *"For the glory of man (is) God...and the receptacle of all His wisdom and power (is) man."* *(A.H. Bk III, 20: 2)*

Once again, one can wonder about the relevance of such teaching for our times. In the twenty-first century, confronted with the damage brought about by sin, it seems difficult to refer to the human body as the place for God's work. In fact, religious history rather bears witness to the difficulties that Christians went through to reconcile salvation with the earthly and bodily human condition. More and more pessimistic views about the body have stifled the enthusiasm and the dynamism of the hope of the early Christians when confronted by the flesh-bearing God. The reason may be that the idea of human beings bound by sin has always been identified with that of 'corrupt flesh.' Is there something relevant for us today

---

16   J. Plagnieux, "La doctrine mariale de saint Irénée" (Saint Irenaeus' Marian Doctrine) *Revue des sciences religieuses,* 44ème année, 1970, p. 182.

in the change of perspective that Irenaeus brought about at the heart of the mystery of the virgin birth? I would like to suggest two reasons for the rehabilitation of the mystery of the virgin birth, as viewed by Irenaeus. The first reason is the rehabilitation of the body as a place for hope. The second one is the importance of keeping the interpretation handed down from Isaiah in which faith recognizes Him in whom its hope dwells, "The lord himself will give you this sign, the virgin shall be with child, and bear a son, and shall name him Emmanuel." (Isaiah 7:14).

To be more specific:

1. How can a Christology, bringing together two opposite signifiers, mother and virgin, open our faith to new potentialities? Doesn't this mean that the body is not closed in on itself, that there is room for what has not yet been said? And, that this 'not yet' of humanity will be filled not only by what comes from the self, but also by what comes from other than the self?

2. If Irenaeus refuses to do away with the contradiction in Isaiah 7:14, it is, indeed, in order to reply to the question with which every Christian is confronted, "But what about you? Who do you say I am?" (Matt. 16:15) In Mary's 'fiat,' human incredulity is replaced by a faith capable of recognizing in Christ the most beautiful fruit born of the will of God and the obedience of the flesh. From this viewpoint all moralizing or mystical argument about virginity is irrelevant. Its true worth, on the symbolical level, is rather to tell us who Jesus is, this man who, in the early history of humanity, opened a new dimension for hope. ∎

CHAPTER IV

He Suffered Under Pontius Pilate, Was Crucified, Died, and Was Buried

A Few Comments About the Vocabulary Dealing with Salvation

In Christian vocabulary, it is almost habitual to say, "He died for our salvation." Without even thinking about it, we link salvation with death. For us the word *salvation* immediately brings to mind the image of the cross, even that of the crucifix.

With Irenaeus we are in quite a different world. As with the Incarnation, the salvation brought about by Christ is to be viewed as part of creation. To speak of salvation is to speak of something essentially positive, i.e. the improvement of what we already are. We need a savior who not only saves us *from* something but *for* something.

The difficulty probably lies in the restricted meaning that we give to the words *savior* and *salvation*, not to mention the word *redemption*. Usually, the vocabulary dealing with salvation only refers to the grim necessity of being saved from sin. A brief reminder of the biblical meaning of the word *salvation* may help us understand the way Irenaeus addressed the issue. The New Testament gives several meanings:

1. The first meaning is simply greetings (*Khaire*), as in "Greet Prisca and Aquila, my fellow workers in Christ Jesus..." (Roman 16:3)

2. A second meaning goes further; *Khaire* may mean 'Rejoice!' The Greek welcome in the Bible is often turned into "May God protect you." This is the kind of peace referred to in the Jewish greeting *shalom*; this is the 'joy' or the 'grace' that the angel wishes Mary (Luke 1:29).

3. A third meaning is the equivalent of the Greek *sôteria*, translated into French as 'salut.' This meaning essentially revolves around the idea of 'keeping in good health,' hence, implicitly being protected against anything that could be a threat. It is therefore clear that the word itself covers a great range of meanings. It does not refer to danger in itself, and even less so to a specific danger.

It seems to me that, with Irenaeus, it is in the widest sense that the word should be understood. When he uses the word *savior* about God or Jesus, he means that their part goes far beyond the forgiveness of sin. By savior, above all, he refers to Him who brings us joy and peace. This is one of Irenaeus' major themes, to see Him who is our salvation, our joy. *"For our face shall see the face of the Lord and shall rejoice with joy unspeakable..." that is to say, "...when it shall behold its own Delight."* (A.H. Bk V, 7: 2)

Even more clearly, Irenaeus sends us back to the joy of Abraham, who rejoiced to see the day of the Lord (Jn 8:56); to the joy of old Simeon, who held God's Salvation in his arms, the light of Nations, and the glory of the people Israel (Luke 2:29-32), and to the exultation of Elizabeth who glorifies God her Savior in the presence of Mary pregnant with Jesus (Luke 1:41-47). One would have to read the whole passage in which Irenaeus identifies salvation with joy without the slightest mention of sin (A.H. Bk IV, 7: 1) in order to understand that even if he agrees with the idea that the Savior has come to save humanity from sin, evil, and death, the fact is that according to Irenaeus, this is not the foremost meaning of salvation, and even less so, the unique meaning.

Another word is closer to the classical meaning of the word *save*, i.e. *redemption*. The Latin translation *redemptio,* from the Greek *lytron,* sends us back to the notion of liberation or more precisely to the *means* of this liberation, or freedom from slavery or captivity. In the Bible, this interpretation is based on the experience of Israel freed from Egypt – and later from captivity in Babylon. In these cases the liberator of Israel is God Himself. He is the Savior of His people. The close link implied here is reinforced by the Hebrew *ga'al* (set free) which refers to family law, according to which the *goël* or close relative is obliged to buy back the members of the family who have become the property of a foreigner.

If God reveals Himself as 'the Redeemer' or 'goël' of His people before the coming of Christ, He reveals Himself as the Redeemer of all by sending His Son. In Christ, the whole of mankind is freed and restored into the family of the Father. This notion of Redemption prevails in the writings of Irenaeus, as we are going to see. We have yet to learn the meaning that he gives to this concept within the overall context of the Revelation. In order to understand Redemption in this overall context, we are going to tackle in detail two important points:

• The fact that we are saved by the whole life of the Incarnate Word and not only in the last moment of His death.

• The fact that the death of Jesus goes far beyond the specific historical framework in order to affect the whole of creation in its spatial and temporal dimensions.

Christ's Entire Life Working for Our Salvation

We are not really used to thinking of Christ's entire life as being our salvation, probably because of the emphasis traditionally put on Saint Paul's teaching about salvation, systematically interpreted over the centuries by Christianity in terms of saving us from evil, "He died for our sins."

To shift the emphasis, without denying Paul's assertion of course, like J.-P. Jossua, [17] I suggest taking the viewpoint of the Bishop of Lyon by going back to the beginning of Jesus' life in order to encompass his whole life on earth – and to see salvation within its full context.

The Incarnate Word saves, by the joy and peace that He brings us in fulfilling our creation, a work made visible by His coming, as well as by the hope He instills in our hearts through His fight to the death against the devil, the enemy of humanity. With Irenaeus, this whole range of meanings is to be kept in mind when dealing with salvation. Before taking up the theme of the death of Jesus as a means of salvation, we are going to look at a few examples drawn from his entire life. Irenaeus sees it as revealing the redeeming power of the Incarnate Word.

In this respect, the themes of companionship (closely linked to that of *accustomization*) and of temptation are characteristic of his thinking.

---

17   J.-P. Jossua, *Le Salut. Incarnation ou mystère pascal,* Paris, Ed. du Cerf, 1968.

The Word seeking the company of humans

Undoubtedly, for Irenaeus, God enjoys the company of human beings. *"He…being the Word of God who dwelt in man and became the Son of man, that He might accustom man to receive God, and God to dwell in man, according to the good pleasure of the Father."* *(A.H. Bk III, 20: 2)*

Even before His advent, the Divine Word had a friendly relationship with humans. *"For just as at that time God spoke to Adam at eventide, searching him out; so in the last times, by means of the same voice, searching out his posterity, He has visited them."* (A.H. Bk V, 15: 4)

What is striking in this text is that the search mentioned concerns Adam *before* the sin. It implies that the search concerning his descendants takes place in the same Adamic context of a God "walking in the garden in the cool of the day." (See Gn 3:8) This impression is confirmed by what Irenaeus says about Abraham who followed the Word in the fullness of his faith, thanks to which he became 'the friend of God.' (A.H. Bk IV, 13: 4)

After His Incarnation, Irenaeus says the same about the disciples who followed their Lord, because the Lord wanted them to be 'friends of God.' What comes out of all this is that friendship between God and humans, between His Word and humans, makes a place for salvation, that is to say, a place where the meeting between humans and God is characterized by the kind of joy which transforms friends. In a way, they convert each other, God getting accustomed to the human way, while human beings open themselves up to God's friendship and get accustomed to receive Him. This is a strikingly bold image for our imagination, but it is quite faithful to Irenaeus' way of thinking. In theological terms, this means that the relationship of friendship and communion is pre-eminent; in other words, human autonomy is always to be respected. It is from within his own freedom that the Word attempts gradually to win humans over.

It seems that Irenaeus is particularly drawn to this theme as he carries it right to the end, recalling the fact that human small-ness inspired God, so to speak, to make Himself small with him. *"It was for this reason that the Son of God, although He was perfect, passed through the state of infancy in common with the rest of man-kind, partaking of it thus not for His own benefit, but for that of the infantile stage of man's existence, in order that man might be able to receive Him." (A.H. Bk IV, 38: 2)*

This fellowship of the Incarnate Word with us brings Irenae-us to an unusual idea that the Lord has sanctified all the ages passing through every stage of human life, until old age. Referring explicitly to Jn 8:56-57, he says that the Lord was close to being fifty, probably the age of maturity for Irenaeus! (See A.H. Bk II, 22: 6) The Lord's care and tenderness thus go very far:

"...not despising or evading any condition of humanity...but sanctifying every age, by that period corresponding to it which be-longed to Himself. For He came to save all through means of Himself – all, I say, who through Him are born again to God – infants, and chil-dren, and boys, and youths, and old men. He therefore passed through every age... Then, at last, He came on to death itself, that He might be the first-born from the dead, that in all things He might have the pre-eminence, the Prince of life, existing before all, and going before all." (A.H. Bk II, 22: 4)

These lines are not made irrelevant here by the Docetic context which compels Irenaeus to insist on the reality of the In-carnation. The entire life of Our Lord is the story of Salvation. By identifying Himself with all the ages through which we are passing,

He sanctified them, that is to say, He transformed them in order to prepare them for incorruptible life initiated by the First-born from the dead.

Irenaeus also implies that the Lord sanctified the various experiences of bodily existence. He recalls the facts that Jesus was hungry; that he was tired at the end of his journeys; that he cried over Lazarus; and that he sweated drops of blood saying, "My soul is overwhelmed with sorrow. *"For all these are tokens of the flesh which had been derived from the earth, which He had recapitulated in Himself, bearing salvation to His own handiwork." (A.H. Bk III, 22: 2)*

Jesus, a human being engaged in a constant struggle against evil

In order to grasp Irenaeus' thinking about salvation, it is necessary to see how he relates it not only to the joy of being accompanied by the Word, but also to the horror of being faced with the presence of evil. But, which evil?

One of the answers to this question is to be found around the ancient figure of the Devil in the Garden. *He* is seen by Irenaeus as the most malevolent and destructive form of evil. As soon as they were created, humans were threatened by this fierce adversary – the one evoked by the Bible in the book of Job (1:6) and in the Apocalypse (12:7-12). Irenaeus does not call into question the reality of his existence. On this point, he simply follows the Scriptures, "Satan by whom all the earth is turned from the right way." (Ap 12: 9) He is the one who lost his place in heaven for 'tempting God,' that is to say, because of an outrageous and disorderly pride he claimed to be on the same level as God. According to Irenaeus, since his fall the 'renegade angel' has been jealous of humans destined to know the happiness that the angel had lost.

In Irenaeus, this image of the Devil from the Scriptures is closely linked to the historical presence of the Son on earth. As soon as He arrived in this world, the devil started putting Him to the test in order to know who He was and ultimately to destroy Him. This new birth threatened his power over humanity, a power of which Adam's sin was the first evidence. The devil therefore tempted Jesus, putting Him to the test and preventing Him from freeing human beings from their own blindness as to their true vocation. This is why the temptations in the desert, narrated by all three synoptic gospels, are already aimed at separating Jesus from God. This is essential here in making our point about the fact that salvation is not restricted to the single event of the Cross. If we admit that Jesus' entire life was marked by the conflict with the forces of evil and that Jesus showed he was a savior each time he chased away the Devil or vanquished the workings of evil in human life, then we can see the epitome of the wider meaning that Irenaeus gave to the idea of salvation in the narrative of the temptations. There is a very thorough exposition in *Against Heresies (Book V, 21-24)*.

In this narrative there is a cosmic dimension to the struggle between good and evil. People's dwellings are distant. The Son is alone, physically weakened by fasting, confronted by the Prince of Darkness the enemy of Good. Let us recall the fact that the Gnostics would not admit a Good God as the creative principle of creation. For them, the creator of the world had to be an inferior and evil being, the devil himself. Of course, from this point of view, the world by its very nature belongs to Satan. Likewise, by their nature, human beings who live in this world would necessarily be the devil's property.

In order to call such teaching into question, Irenaeus attempts to overturn the image. The devil has no power over the world because the latter does not belong to him. It belongs to God and when His Son comes into the world, He comes into His own world. (See *"To His own things He came." A.H. Bk V, 18: 2*) The devil is thus an intruder. Worse, he is a liar because he tried to make the first human beings believe that the world belonged to him and that it was under his power. Throughout history, he instilled false ideas in humans about their relationship with God, ideas which prevented them from seeing the truth of the Love of God for them.

Given all this, it is obvious that temptation comes from the devil who is stronger than humans because of his guile. Who would save them by showing them the duplicity of such a treacherous enemy? A stronger one than the devil would be needed to come and unmask his deceitfulness. Irenaeus says, he stands more and more violently against humanity (*A.H. Bk V, 24: 4*). The 'strong man' is, of course, Jesus. He is the strong man according to Matthew 12:29. He engages in combat with the devil to loosen the chains that hold humans in the grip of a thief – Satan who tried to wrench humans away from God (*A.H Bk V, 21: 3*). By his refusal to tempt God, to believe in the proud lies of the devil, Jesus overcomes the fallen angel who prevented human beings from knowing *themselves* as the image of God, and hence, to depart from their fulfillment.

What can we conclude about this way of dealing with the temptations of Jesus? There are two specific points to bear in mind:

• The idea that the victory of Jesus over the demon in the desert was no mere prelude to His victory over death and to His resurrection. It was already the work of salvation as the true knowledge capable of unmasking the Devil's lies which keep humans in ignorance.

• The idea that one must resist the pessimistic view according to which the world belongs to the inexorable forces of evil.

As for the first point, the meaning that Irenaeus gives to salvation in the narrative of the temptations, sends us back to the idea that human beings are freed by the true knowledge of who they are. God's word, by which Jesus overcame Satan, reveals to humans that they are deeply mistaken when they consider themselves as the sole and unique masters of their destiny. Such blindness is costly, and sometimes very costly. This prevents them from fulfilling the true aim of their lives, that is to say, to become what they are, the image of God. The salvation that we are dealing with here is that of a liberation brought about by the humble recognition that we belong to God. To refuse to recognize this truth is to close in on oneself and to lock oneself into the power of evil.

As for the second point, the rejection of a pessimistic attitude towards the world, it reinforces the idea, often referred to here and explicitly asserted by Irenaeus, that God uses His own creation for 'the salvation of man.' (*A.H. Bk V, 18: 1*) It is in this world that humans gradually become aware of the meaning of their own lives, an awareness which is already a form of salvation when it bears the imprint of its divine author.

In all this, we have seen nothing that would suggest that salvation is the result of an act of expiation or the substitution of an innocent victim for a human sinner! Irenaeus gives us a different outlook on salvation, broader than usual, by giving a redeeming dimension to everything the Son did in his life as well as in his death. Then what remains to be dealt with is the question of the salvation brought about by Jesus in particular at the end of his life on earth.

In What Sense Are We Saved By The Death of Jesus?

It should be clear by now that Irenaeus views the death of Jesus within the broader context of salvation. For him the question, "At what precise moment did the Lord save us?" would miss the point. This having been said, he undoubtedly gives the crucifixion a redeeming dimension which is indispensable because it is the last of these many redeeming moments (*A.H. Bk V, 16-20*).

The function of the language of atonement in Irenaeus

When Irenaeus speaks of redemption specifically referring to the act by which Jesus gave himself to death so that we might live, he draws directly on Paul's language. It is no surprise for us since Paul is the theologian 'par excellence' concerning the tenet of the redeeming death of Christ.

The risk of misunderstanding the bishop of Lyon is thus real, if we do not put his assertions, clearly inspired from Paul, within the appropriate context. Let us address the issue in two parts, firstly with the text of Romans 5:12, then with the language of atonement.

The text of Romans 5:12

In this text, we can assert confidently that the name 'Adam' refers to a typology and not a character from history. For Paul, as for Irenaeus, Adam represents humankind in its sinful dimension, consistent with the sin which goes back to the first human being. A parallel is drawn between Adam, as humankind, and Christ in order to put them in opposition. Yet, the parallel is not a symmetrical one.

Romans 5:12 explicitly asserts that death came into this world because of sin. "Well then, it was through one man that *sin came into the world*, and through sin – death, and thus death has spread through the whole human race because everyone has sinned."

One usually sees here a causal relationship. On the one hand, death came into this world because of sin, and on the other hand because of that very sin, all human beings have become sinners. As for Irenaeus, he does not mention the issue of a sinful humankind being part of the sin of the first human being (he did not have the Latin translation that we know, which is a later version). In fact, Irenaeus well understands the implication of the typological parallel in Romans 5:12 where Paul implies, without making it explicit, that if by 'one man' sin and death entered into this world, the idea should be pursued by saying that by 'one man' justice and life came into this world. This is precisely what Irenaeus does.

With him, the coherence of the Adam-Christ parallel typology becomes explicit. Here is the full passage on this issue *"For as by one man's disobedience sin entered, and death obtained (a place) through sin; so also by the obedience of one man, righteousness having been introduced, shall cause life to fructify in those persons who in times past were dead."* (A.H. Bk III, 21: 10)

In all this we are unquestionably in a context in which salvation is the issue, but with Irenaeus this context is always to be seen in a wider perspective, that of the understanding of the person of Christ. In order to assert both the reality of the incarnation of the Word and the grandeur of Its mission, Irenaeus was led to contrast the work of Christ with that of humanity. The two Adams, a Pauline theme, enable Irenaeus to think of his teaching in terms of opposite pairs: Adam-Christ, disobedience-obedience, sin-grace, and death-life. But, according to this typology, the 'original sin' is not what is at stake since Irenaeus does not know the phrase. In other words, the sin of the first human being was not so serious a sin as to cause all

Adam's descendants to be personally and indelibly marked. Nowhere in his writings does he say that we are directly marked by the sin of an historical man.

This being said, Irenaeus does not call into question Genesis 3. He accepts perfectly the idea that the first human being sinned and bore the consequences of this act. Nothing could be clearer than that Adam's descendants should be sinners too. It can even be said that their own sins validated, in some way, the sin of the first human being. But, Adam is not the cause of their sins.

Perhaps to clarify the core of Irenaeus' thinking on this issue, we might go back to the difficult text of Romans 5:12 and say that "all men sin with Adam", and not, "in whom all men have sinned". In other words, they are a race of sinners of whom Adam was the first link in the chain.

In brief, Irenaeus does not seek to account for the presence of sin in humankind as a result of Adam's sin. He does not explain anything. He notes that we are all sinners and that the first sinner, Adam, was the least culpable as he did not know how to defend himself against Satan. In this context Adam could be viewed as the permanent dimension of sin in humankind.

But, once again, in all this, Irenaeus makes Christ our essential focus. Adam has given Irenaeus a means to speak about the reality of the incarnation. In everything he says about Adam, the main character is the second Adam, or rather the principle of the Adamic race, the Incarnate Word. Hence, sin and its consequences are serious but are no match in comparison with the grandeur of Christ's achievement.

However, there are still some reflections on atonement in Irenaeus that do not directly involve Romans 5:12 but which are worth mentioning here.

The language of atonement in Irenaeus

The way Irenaeus draws from Paul in what he says about atonement is undeniable. There is thus an obligation for us not to seek too quickly another meaning than the one Irenaeus himself would have given to the well-known formulations: 'forgiveness of sins,' 'remission of our debt,' 'he gave his life as a ransom,' etc.

To start with, it is interesting to note that Irenaeus uses this language without any comment. Because his focus is somewhere else, he always wants to say who Christ is. He wants to identify the one who cured the born-blind and who vanquished the devil in the desert, with the one who died on the cross. This human, who proved to be so strong in this unfinished world and against evil, is really the Son sent by the Father:

"But as our Lord alone is truly Master, so the Son of God is truly good and patient, the Word of God the Father having been made the Son of man. For He fought and conquered; for He was man contending for the fathers, and through obedience doing away with disobedience completely; for He bound the strong man, (Satan) and set free the weak, and endowed His own handiwork with salvation, by destroying sin." (A.H. Bk III, 18: 6)

How are we to understand this text? Looking at it from a theological point of view, it seems to me that the underlying meaning is always the same: to say who Christ is. This language of atonement and of debt becomes even clearer when viewed in keeping with the theology of the Word in the gospel according to John. Therefore, a delicate balance appears and helps to qualify what seemed to be an excessively legal stance on redemption.

Before His coming, the Word had known humans enslaved by their ignorance. After his coming he knew them as disciples. In a beautiful text from *Against Heresies, Book IV 14: 1* inspired by Jesus' farewell in Saint John, Irenaeus says that salvation is to follow Jesus who is the light of the disciple. It is clear in this text that the light that he speaks about is that of the Son, the light of Truth freeing human beings from ignorance of the identity of the Word and from ignorance of their own dignity as friends of the Word. *Salvation*, the freedom that the Lord brought about in his own life on earth, was not limited to freedom from sin but also from ignorance. *Redemption*, according to Irenaeus, affects humans in their intelligence as well as in their moral dimension.

From these reflections on the vocabulary of atonement, we shall conclude that:

• Sin is not 'sufficient cause' for the coming of Christ. Sin revealed the dimension of struggle, of fatigue, and of fighting in the mission of the Incarnate Word, but it was not the major cause for His coming.

• There is no theology of expiation in Irenaeus; the idea of atonement is closer to the idea of liberation.

• The outcome of the battle between Jesus and Satan was not a foregone conclusion. It was not automatically determined by the victory of the Son. As a human being, a point that Irenaeus constantly insists upon, Jesus did not have divine power at his disposal. As a true member of our human race, His triumph over sin and death was a true victory.

Seen from this perspective, Jesus' death is not to be thought of as a sacrifice offered to God but as the entry of Jesus into the struggle against the forces of evil which enslave humans. Jesus fulfills his mission right to the end, leading the battle where human beings are held prisoners, that is to say in the kingdom of death.

So how are we to understand Jesus' death on the cross from this specific viewpoint?

Christ hung upon the tree: the spatial dimension of salvation

The cross where Jesus was hung for his death is to be seen within the context of the cosmic cross. Jesus' crucifixion is the visible sign of the recapitulation enacted by the invisible Word.

All these themes are closely linked in this very good example of Irenaeus' synthesizing views:

"For the Creator of the world is truly the Word of God; and this is our Lord, who in the last times was made man, existing in this world, and who in an invisible manner contains all things created, and is inscribed in the shape of a cross [or inherent] in the entire creation, since the Word of God governs and arranges all things; and therefore, He came to His own in a visible manner, and was made flesh, and hung upon the tree, that He might sum up all things in Himself." (A.H. Bk V, 18: 3)

It is difficult to imagine anything more unexpected. In that section of *Against Heresies* explicitly devoted to the crucifixion (*A.H. Bk V, 16: 3-20*), we find an extraordinary conjunction of themes: creation, divine providence, cosmic cross, incarnation, universal salvation, crucifixion and recapitulation. It thus can be seen that Jesus' death has no meaning per se, separated from God's design as a whole. This unity is revealed in the unity of the invisible Word and the visible Lord. It is thanks to this unity of identity that His obedience till death is capable of destroying the chains of our disobedience. Only He could reconcile sinners with the Father, since from the beginning, He was there with disobedient human beings while Himself a member of humanity.

In all this, there is not a hint of dolorism or psychologism. The physical reality of Jesus' passion and death and his state of mind or the intensity of his suffering are not the focus of Irenaeus' theological approach. These concerns, along with the terrifying aspects of Jesus' death, belong to a much later tradition, particularly those of the mystics in the fourteenth century. Irenaeus' concern is rather to show how the cross on which our Lord, who is our Life, was hung meant that all is finally in the Hands of God. Nothing escapes Him.

The very shape of the cross conveys this meaning for Irenaeus. Its verticality makes us look upward to heaven, towards the seat of our hope. Its horizontality, with both arms of the cross, makes us look to the two peoples, the Jews and the Gentiles, scattered to the ends of the earth.

"By means of a tree again was it [the Word] made manifest to all, showing the height, the length, the breadth, the depth in itself; and, as a certain man among our predecessors observed... "Through the extension of the hands of a divine person, gathering together the two peoples to one God." For these were two hands, because there were two peoples scattered to the ends of the earth; but there was one head in the middle, as there is but one God, who is above all, and through all, and in us all." (A.H. Bk V, 17: 4)

In this magnificent vision of the cross, we have what I call *the spatial dimension* of salvation. The Lord, hung before us with wide-open arms to gather the whole of humanity together, is the manifestation of His vocation to reconcile the different peoples scattered throughout the world. It is by means of the cross that the Author of the world makes the universality of His Love visible in an undeniable way. From now on, He speaks to our hope through the visible forms and figures fixed in space, in creation. More precisely, the Son had to fulfill His work through the shape of a cross to ensure that His coming was for the whole of humanity.

"The Word of God Almighty, who in unseen wise in our midst is universally extended in all the world, and encompasses its length and breadth and height and depth (for by the Word of God the whole universe is ordered and disposed) in it is crucified the Son of God, inscribed crosswise upon it all…for it is right that He being made visible, should set upon all things visible the sharing of His cross, that He might show His operation on visible things through a visible form." (Dem. 34)

This passage from Irenaeus' *Demonstration of the Apostolic Preaching* echoes what he says in *Against Heresies* (A.H. Bk V, 17: 4), which we have just seen. This shows the utmost importance of the theme for him. But, we find something more going back to the Epistle to the Ephesians, the most obvious source of the four dimensions of the work of the Son: "And may you have the power to understand, as all God's people should, how wide, how long, how high, and how deep his love is. May you experience the love of Christ, though it is too great to understand fully. Then you will be made complete with all the fullness of life and power that comes from God." (Ephesians 3: 18-19)

What is striking in Paul is that the four dimensions of the mystery of the love of Christ, which take us into God's plenitude, refer to the universal work of the Son in time and space – and yet, without the slightest reference to the cross. The four dimensions of the mystery of Christ – in other words, His universality – are applied to the cross by Irenaeus, and not by Paul. What is the meaning of this presentation?

The key is to be found, I think, in the universality of Ephesians 3. Paul asserts that the Gentiles and the prophets were given the same Promise as we, the 'ecclesia,' thanks to the unfathomable richness of Christ, hidden for centuries in God and now made manifest in his Christ. If for Irenaeus the width, the length, the height and the depth of this great Design of God conjure up the shape of the cross, it becomes impossible to restrict salvation to the historical cross erected a few hundred yards from the gates of Jerusalem during the Jewish Passover. It is even less possible to restrict the cross to the specific fact of the crucifixion with all that it implies in the spirituality of suffering and expiation.

What is the symbolism of the four dimensions of this image? By bringing together the length and the width of Christ's salvation, the cross extends its arms horizontally to the end of the world to include the whole of humanity. It reveals the *universality* of God's design. By bringing together the height and the depth of salvation vertically, it reveals the unity of this design, that is to say, the *intrinsic link between creation and redemption.* The symbol of the cross makes us know what Paul calls the fullness of God's Plenitude. In Him, both human and divine actions come together in order to show us that we are made, not for death, but for life. Life triumphs over death.

Look up to Christ, the Word, 'hung upon the tree' to redeem us and give us life. He is not our death, but our life held before our eyes. At the very heart of the image of death, is revealed its ultimate meaning which is life.

The cross does not belong to the realm of causality or necessity. It introduces us to the dimension of gift, grace, and Love. As a signifier, the cross points to a wider meaning than itself which Irenaeus sums up into one word, *recapitulation.*

Christ the Recapitulator: the temporal dimension of salvation

The death of Christ under Pontius Pilate is an historical fact for Irenaeus as well as for us; but, with him, the historical cross loses much of its factual nature because of its importance in Christ's work of recapitulation. The Greek word comes from Ephesians 1:10, "to be put into effect when the times reach their fulfillment – to bring together (to recapitulate) all things in heaven and on earth under Christ."

The reference to Paul is thus clear, but Irenaeus' theological work sharpens its focus. On the one hand, the Recapitulator is Christ Himself; and on the other hand, in order to fulfill His task, his main objective is the recapitulation of Adam. The idea may come as a surprise to us, but it is pre-eminent. If the first human being is lost, how could humankind following in Adam's footsteps be saved? He, who has recapitulated all things in Himself, has also recapitulated – and even firstly – God's original work, Adam. Christ, the perfect replica, or even better the 'true Adam,' has included in Himself the first human being who, by his disobedience, launched humankind on the path of sin and death. With the victory of the perfect human, imperfect Adam finds himself relaunched on the path of life which reaffirms his creation in the image and likeness of God.

"So then the Lord, summing up afresh this man, (Adam) took the same dispensation of entry into flesh, being born from the Virgin by the Will and the Wisdom of God; that He also should show forth the likeness of Adam's entry into flesh and there should be that which was written in the beginning, man after the image and likeness of God." (Dem.32)

Here again, we come across Irenaeus' comprehensive viewpoint. He does not consider any aspect of the Christian revelation in isolation. His gift for encompassing the whole of humanity enables him to think of the work of Christ in terms of recapitulation where all human beings in space and time, from first to last, are brought together in Christ.

"When He became incarnate, and was made man, He commenced afresh the long line of human beings...stooping low, even to death, and consummating the arranged plan of our salvation." (A.H. Bk III, 18: 1-2)

Somehow it can be said that recapitulation is the work of Christ par excellence, a work made visible during his life on earth. From His birth to His glorification, through His passion and death, He encompasses all humanity. He sums up and gives meaning to all divine interventions on the side of humans in space and time.

Yet, a question may be asked: what is there to recapitulate if human beings have never escaped the Hands of God, a strongly held assertion in Irenaeus? The question is all the more relevant as Irenaeus says that the Lord has become flesh and blood *"recapitulating in Himself not a certain other, but that original handiwork of the Father, seeking out that thing which had perished."* (A.H. Bk V, 14: 2)

Negatively, it can be said that humans were never lost in the sense that the change they underwent in their lifetime as sinners would be a change of status, a substantial downfall. One would not understand how the Word could really share such corporeality! The loss concerns the human (*anthropos*) who has lost, so to speak, the habit of behaving with dignity in the image of God. It is by reasserting this human dignity, by contemplating the perfect human, hung upon the tree that the human is taken in hand, saved, in a word, 'recapitulated.'

Positively, recapitulation is not only the recovery of what was lost, in the sense that we have just seen, but also the rehabilitation of human beings as the image of God to a degree of perfection that had never been reached before the Incarnation. The word *recapitulation* evokes the idea of salvation bringing together all into one: *"In one alone, all things, all are united. Salvation, asserted once and for all by the raising of the cross above all things, is essentially what Christ envisioned when he wished like a mother-hen to bring his people to Him, 'How often would I have gathered your children together, and you would not' (Matt 23:37) a passage which Irenaeus quotes within the context of liberty."* (A.H. Bk IV, 37: 1)

Recapitulation is thus not a work done automatically, independently of the human will. To be gathered together, all united in one, Christ is, I think, the meaning of salvation in recapitulation.

As it so happens, there was a sinner who seemed to be really beyond saving, even for Irenaeus. As we have just seen, it is not at all the case with Adam, who was saved, who never escaped the Hands of God, even if he had lost the sense of his dignity. Rather, we are dealing with Cain. With him, we have the example of the truly unrepentant sinner. Contrary to Adam, Cain is not at all ready to repent. Faced with his hard and impenetrable heart, Irenaeus seems to be really troubled. He encounters in Cain one of the most enigmatic, indecipherable facets of sin. He cannot close his eyes to the fact that there are apparently sinners who are deaf to any call to conversion. Irenaeus does not know what to say about the unrepentant who coldly maintain their sin. But what sin? The murder of Abel, of course. It was abominable that Cain should have slain his brother. But, with Irenaeus the mystery of evil, persistent, impervious to grace, does not lie there. It is in the sinner's refusal of God's mercy that Irenaeus sees the horror of sin.

"For if it is wicked to slay a brother, much worse is it thus insolently and irreverently to reply to the omniscient God as if he could battle Him. And for this he did himself bear a curse about with him, because he gratuitously brought an offering of sin, having had no reverence for God, nor being put to confusion by the act of fratricide." (A.H. Bk III, 23: 4)

For Irenaeus, there was something deliberate and inflexible in Cain's behavior, a kind of pride that he did not find in Adam. Irenaeus seems to say that the seriousness of Cain's sin was of an entirely different kind. He had time to ponder over his crime, even to add sin to sin as Irenaeus says, "added sin to sin". (*A.H. Bk III, 23: 4*) For this reason, he did not sin inadvertently like Adam and Eve. On the contrary, Cain acted as if he believed it possible to deceive God Himself. He acted fully, of his own free will, whereas...

"The case of Adam, however, had no analogy with this, but was altogether different. For, having been beguiled by another under the pretext of immortality, he is immediately seized with terror, and hides himself; not as if he were able to escape from God; but rather, in a state of confusion at having transgressed his command. He feels unworthy to appear before and to hold converse with God." (A.H. Bk III, 23: 5)

Irenaeus shows tenderness and an astonishing understanding of Adam who was almost caught unaware by his sin. Whereas concerning Cain, he wonders why the pedagogical dimension of sin, which gives the experience of evil its bitterness, was unable to touch the heart of the murderer. *"To God's question, "Where is your brother?" – a carefully designed question aimed at stirring the sinner's conscience – Cain refused to 'soften.'" (A.H. Bk III, 23: 4)* The idea also crops up somewhere else, in another context: *"According to your hardness and impenitent heart, you store to yourself wrath against the*

day of wrath, and the revelation of the righteous judgment of God."
(A.H. Bk IV, 37: 1)

Faced with such heartlessness, Irenaeus does not really know what to think, but he only indirectly replies to our question: Why is it so? Why do some people seem to be impervious to divine pedagogy wishing to bring humanity to know what is good through the unhappy experience of sin? Indeed, Irenaeus acknowledges the brotherhood of sinners from Adam to the last members of the human race, but he seems to say that the sinful condition of mankind is more due to Satan than to Adam. The latter overestimated his capacities, but never did he show the pride of Satan. In his case, God's inquiry certainly provoked childish excuses, but not Cain's insolent cry of defiance: "Am I my brother's keeper?" (*A.H. Bk III, 23: 4; Gn 4:9*) To a second question, "Was Cain condemned to hell?" Irenaeus does not reply directly either. The issue of eternal damnation will be addressed further on. For the moment, we are concerned with viewing Cain in the context of the salvation carried out by Christ in terms of recapitulation.

It seems that Cain's refusal, his liberty, does not define the very nature of the human race. It is the refusal of an individual. The Lord, fighting against Satan to the end, till death, shows that the human race is not tainted or corrupt. Rather, it is frail, enslaved by ignorance and vanity, hence able to be rehabilitated by the Hand of the Creator, that is to say, 'recapitulated' without losing its freedom. Seen from this perspective, liberty is not denied, but it is threatened by a lack of wisdom, by the limitations of its nature, which is lacking self-control because it is inhabited by desires that do not accord with its own reality when it is at its best.

And that is true for everybody, we are all capable of evil or good.

"But if some had been made by nature bad, and others good, these latter would not be deserving of praise for being good, for such were they created; nor would the former be reprehensible, for thus they were made (originally). But since all men are of the same nature, able both to hold fast and to do what is good; and, on the other hand, having also the power to cast it from them and not to do it." (A.H. Bk IV, 37: 2)

In this, we have another reason for the universal recapitulation of the Lord: since anyone is capable of sinning, in the same way, anyone else – whether a sinner or a saint – has a place in this great work through which the Son inscribes the sign of the cross in the entire creation. All are recapitulated, even if some freely refuse to assert their belonging to Christ. ■

CHAPTER V

HE DESCENDED TO THE DEAD, ON THE THIRD DAY HE ROSE AGAIN, HE ASCENDED TO HEAVEN AND IS SEATED AT THE RIGHT HAND OF GOD, THE FATHER ALMIGHTY

THE READER MIGHT BE SURPRISED TO SEE 'DESCENT TO THE DEAD' linked with the Resurrection. In fact, we usually leave open the enigmatic notion as that of Jesus' descending into an indefinable place before moving straight to the Passover. This is not Irenaeus' way. For him, this descent is meaningful and necessary to reveal the absolute victory of Christ. Thus, we are going to look into the way Irenaeus thought about this issue before moving on to the Resurrection itself.

UNFINISHED BEINGS, THE DEAD AWAIT

Irenaeus writings on this subject

To begin with, let us recall a few words from the First Epistle of Peter: "He went and made proclamation to the imprisoned spirits – to those who were disobedient long ago when God waited patiently in the days of Noah while the ark was being built..." (1P 3:19-20)

A certain number of the Church Fathers understood this preaching to the dead by Christ as a straightforward proclamation of his victory over the powers of hell.

A greater number of them saw in this a statement of universal salvation. If the dead, even those who lived before Jesus, are called back to life, we then know that nobody is excluded from salvation. the 'descent to the dead' is a way of saying that the victory of Christ is absolute since it includes all human beings from the beginning to the end. His victory, which is the basis of our hope, of our trust in Him, begins with those who had least reason to hope, those who lived and died before the coming of Christ.

Irenaeus clearly shared the latter viewpoint. He refers several times to the visit made by Christ to the sleeping dead in the dark regions of the earth. Let us specify though, that, for him, this is not 'the devil's hell' but what is called *sheol* in Hebrew, an underworld that is under God's sovereignty (see Acts 2:27). In the Semitic view, a human being deprived of its *nephesh* or 'living soul' did not cease to exist, but was carried to Sheol as a *human being* and not specifically as a soul. Irenaeus first mentioned this in a passage in Book IV (*Against Heresies*) where he recalls a certain number of signs by Jesus meant to free humans from their servitude, from different forms of servitude such as sin and death. He thought for instance of the last Supper and of the disciples *lying* on sofas. After having washed their feet, he gave them the bread of life: his own body. This image of the disciples recumbent before the table of the Last Supper elicits in Irenaeus the image of all the others lying under the earth, in death, awaiting the life that Jesus will bring to them:

"He administered food to them in a recumbent posture, indicating that those who were lying in the earth were those to whom He came to impart life. As Jeremiah declares, "The holy Lord remembered

His dead Israel, who slept in the land of sepulture; and He descended to them to make known to them His salvation, that they might be saved." *(A.H. Bk IV, 22: 1)*

The text, which Irenaeus attributes to Jeremiah does not belong to the canonical books. It is only known by the quotes made by Justin and Irenaeus. Whatever the source or origin of the text, one thing is clear: Irenaeus was convinced that the Jewish people were living in the hope of the resurrection. A little further on, he mentions the disciples sleeping during the passion of Christ in the garden. And, he clearly shows that he thinks once more not only of them but also of those who were locked into the prison of death – even those who were put to the test "when God waited patiently," as the epistle of Peter says:

"...the Lord found them sleeping, He let it pass – thus indicating the patience of God in regard to the state of slumber in which men lay; but coming the second time, He aroused them, and made them stand up, in token that His passion is the arousing of His sleeping disciples on whose account 'He also descended into the lower parts of the earth,' to behold with His eyes the state of those who were resting from their labors... For it was not merely for those who believed in Him in the time of Tiberius Caesar that Christ came, nor did the Father exercise His providence for only the men who are now alive, but for all men altogether, who from the beginning, according to their capacity, in their generation have both loved God, and practised justice and piety towards their neighbours..." *(A.H. Bk IV, 22: 1-2).*

Irenaeus makes a second allusion to the dead visited by Christ in Book V of *Against Heresies* where he mentions the end of time. He makes a very close link between the resurrection of the Just and that of Christ, unsurprisingly so, since it is absolutely essential to faith. But, what is interesting for him is, above all, the fact that the

Resurrection involves the body. If Christ descended into the lower parts of the earth, it was in order to reassure the dead of His power over death and to tell them that they will come to life again, an incorruptible life, thanks to the First-born from the dead. The victory of Christ over death will be made manifest on the third day, by means of His resurrection in the flesh: proof and sign of the incorruptibility of every life recapitulated by him, whatever its historic manifestation in space and time. This again is a doctrine of hope which Irenaeus wants to set against the Gnostics' pessimism, those who deny the resurrection of the flesh. He insists on the idea that Christ spent three days with the dead before his resurrection. And this, in order to refute the Gnostics for whom the elected do not need time to reach heavenly life. They are perfect before death. This is why the Gnostics think that, as soon as they are dead, they will ascend to heaven without resurrection.

Irenaeus opposes this idea saying:

"For they do not choose to understand, that if these things are as they say, the Lord Himself, in whom they profess to believe, did not rise again upon the third day; but immediately upon His expiring on the cross, undoubtedly departed on high, leaving His body to the earth. But the case was that for three days He dwelt in the place where the dead were, He descended to them, to rescue and save them." (A.H. Bk V, 31: 1)

Three lessons

What can we learn from Irenaeus' teaching about 'Christ's descent to the dead?' I can see at least three things to keep in mind:

1. The word *hell*. Irenaeus does not use the word *hell* to refer to the place where the dead await salvation, their Savior. For him, the place where Christ went after his death is the place where the dead

await resurrection. This is why he refers to this place as 'the land of sepulture' or 'the lower parts of the earth.' Nowhere does he use the word *hell* to speak of the period of time between the death of Christ and his resurrection. Hence, for him it is simply about our earth, the earth which bears us all our life, which is our shelter after death until the resurrection.

2. A symbolic approach. As in the Bible itself, Irenaeus uses symbolic language to help people understand about faith. He knows very well that there is no image to convey adequately our hope of resurrection. One notes that, with him, words always evoke more than the simple literal meaning. Rather, they open up an area of meaning, thanks to which, a new reading becomes possible.

Let us recall the example from the texts that we have just read: the image of being laid out. First, it was about the disciples being recumbent before the table of the Last Supper and nourished by the bread of life. They received food and strength from the hand of the very One who was their Life.

Then a little further on, Irenaeus evokes the image of these same disciples lying on the ground in the garden, fast asleep during the passion of the Lord. But, they are not left sleeping because the Lord wakes them and makes them stand up. Irenaeus explains that Christ, in this way, indicates the fruit of his suffering: the awakening of humanity after the sleep of death and its being made to stand up forever by the resurrection. This is perfectly in keeping with Irenaeus' idea that 'Man fully alive' is, above all, 'humanity standing up,' humans awakened and nourished by the Lord so that they might set themselves on the path to neverending life.

Finally, Irenaeus evokes the image of those laid out in the sleep of death. They are lying in the land of the sepulcher, waiting for the food of the Word, waiting for the words preached by Christ himself proclaiming their liberation from the prison of death. The Lord had also to go to his own who had preceded him and who awaited the good news of the Resurrection. The dead too must be put back on their feet to stand up and follow Christ on the way to life, on the way leading to incorruptible life.

One can see here how Irenaeus proceeds. The image of 'being laid out' works to suggest deeper meaning. One way or another, the body lying down connotes the idea of a certain weakness, a lack of vitality. During the Last Supper, the Lord gives the bread of life to his recumbent disciples, because of their need for food which was not only physical but also spiritual. Lying on the ground in the garden, they have to stand up to face life and stand in this world as if already resurrected. Finally, Christ makes the dead stand up by bringing them the good news of their imminent resurrection.

To truly understand Irenaeus, one must always take into account the way in which he proceeds. For him, the Christian faith is not a series of dogmatic rules more or less separate, or compartmentalized. Faith is essentially faith in someone: Christ in all that he was and all that he did. To mention just one of Christ's actions gives Irenaeus the opportunity to remind us that everything Christ did had one single purpose, our salvation. This is why for example, Irenaeus does not hesitate to speak of the Eucharist, while discussing death and resurrection. In this there is no incoherence, but on the contrary the deep underlying logic of everything done by Christ. This accounts for Irenaeus' constant concern to bring everything back to Him.

3. The unfinished state of the dead. A third and last point, let us notice that Irenaeus says that the Lord is concerned with the unfinished beings of creation. The word *unfinished* here is quite unexpected, even surprising, as we tend to think that everything ends

with death. Everything will be over at our last breath. There will be no possibility for progress, for growth in faith, hope and love. This is what we often heard in our catechism classes.

Irenaeus does not share this viewpoint. He clearly states that we are still unfinished even after death. We shall see further on how he speaks of death itself as a kind of threshold we get across to get to God faster. Death is nothing else for him than the removal of obstacles, especially of sin, which prevent us from living fully the life of God. We shall come back to this. For the moment, what we need to underscore is the fact that, with Irenaeus, death does not put an end to our hope for progress, for going further into our understanding and love of God. Much to the contrary, we are the unfinished creatures of creation, even after death. God, in his patience, acknowledges that we need time to fully become what we are, His image and likeness. This is why the Lord spent three days among the dead, says Irenaeus ('time,' even after death!). The dead also need time to welcome and understand the implications of the Good News proclaimed by the Lord! For the dead too, he must open 'the Scriptures' as he did to the disciples on the road to Emmaus.

These three points show us clearly how Irenaeus is faithful to his initial insights which govern his thinking. The themes of growth, recapitulation, and of Christ as the principle of humanity are particularly present here. The idea that created beings always need time to be truly in the image and likeness of God is compared with God's patience which goes beyond death. The idea too that the Lord has recapitulated the whole of mankind from its beginnings by descending to the dead is compared with the idea of Christ, principle of creation, who has lost nothing that is His.

This is how I understand this difficult lesson in the Creed concerning Christ's stay among the dead. It is an approach which highlights symbols in religious discourse. I think that it is the best way of dealing with Irenaeus' way of thinking, as it is an approach that he himself used. It is true that in his writings there is no theory of symbols, but symbolism is constantly at work there. And, in other words, he is right as he knows that the religious discourse is not a language of empirical proofs, but one of spiritual meaning.

The question remains as to whether this approach is still relevant for us today. Is it still possible for people today, who have lost touch with the former way of using symbols, especially biblical and cosmo-biological, to restore this teaching in order to deepen their own faith? Are people today too steeped in rationalism and empiricism to grasp the breadth of a language using figures of speech and symbols? Not only is the question interesting but also pressing today. How to proceed, especially when talking about the resurrection, first and foremost, that of Jesus' resurrection from among the dead? Are we so limited by the way we think that we can only see the word as the exact equivalent of the thing it refers to? Especially when it is about resurrection, are we reduced to arguments based on crude materialism, because we no longer know how to view it within a broader scope than that of a corpse resuscitated from the sepulcher?

ALIVE

The Risen

Now familiar with Irenaeus' approach, we are not surprised to see that, in his writing there is no commentary dealing with the Resurrection. He asserts the truth of this article of faith throughout his work but nowhere does he explain it. Nowhere does he speak of 'evidence,' 'proof,' or how it happened. With a very firm theological grasp, he focused on the *why* of the event. This is why I would rather speak of the Risen rather than the Resurrection as such. Irenaeus is not interested in the event itself but in what happens around it.

Let us take a text that best exemplifies Irenaeus' method for meditating on the Risen. In Book III of *Against Heresies*, Irenaeus asserts with Peter, in his speech on Whitsunday, that Christ is risen (Ac. 2:24).

Then, he immediately moves on to the meaning of a fact, which he deals with, not as something unheard of, strange, or incongruous, but rather as an event consistent with God's overall design. The Resurrection is part of the reasoning about the incorruptibility for which human beings are destined. Recalling Peter's words in Acts 2:31-33, Irenaeus says that the prophet David 'spoke of the resurrection of Christ, that He was not left in hell, neither did His flesh see corruption.' This Jesus, he said, *"Hath God raised up, of which we all are witnesses: who, being exalted by the right hand of God, receiving from the Father the promise of the Holy Ghost, hath shed forth this gift which ye now see and hear." (A.H. Bk III, 12: 2)*

It is all there: the father who raised Jesus, the latter exalted in glory; the love poured out in our hearts by the Holy Spirit; and David, the figure of humankind waiting, prophesying that people born of our kind will not see corruption. If Christ is the focus of this text, he is not alone, he does not even act all by himself, on his own authority. Irenaeus explicitly says two important things:

1. It is God who 'raised him up,' 'this Jesus, hath God raised up,' the Son who died on the cross is brought back to life by God.

2. He has been exalted by the right hand of God. Acts 2:33 was quoted by Irenaeus referring to the psalm: "exalted by the right hand of God, receiving from the Father the promise of the Holy

Ghost…" It is by the power of the Father that the Son is glorified, exalted after his resurrection.

It is at the beginning of Book V of *Against Heresies* that we find Irenaeus' most elaborate thinking on the resurrection, not just that of Jesus but of all the dead. In fact, it is impossible to consider one without the other: all of Irenaeus' efforts are focused on the idea that the corporeal resurrection of Christ is the warranty of our own. *"In the same manner, therefore, as Christ did rise in the substance of flesh, and pointed out to His disciples the mark of the nails and the opening in His side…so "shall He also," it is said, "raise us up by His own power." (A.H. Bk V, 7: 1)*

Bearing in mind the close connection that Irenaeus makes between Jesus' resurrection and our own, and being thus true to his way of thinking, I'll start dealing with the article, "I believe in the resurrection of the flesh," which is actually at the end of the Creed even though I will go back to it in the last chapter.

The way in which the Son makes himself accessible to all humans

My aim is to put Irenaeus' thinking within a clearly universal framework. The Resurrection of the Son is the indispensable crowning of his work on earth, but at the same time the manifestation of his universal worth. Here is what Irenaeus says on the subject: *"The Son resurrected from the dead, as being the first begotten in all the creation, the Son of God being made the Son of man, that through Him we may receive the adoption – humanity sustaining and receiving and embracing the Son of God." (A.H. Bk III, 16: 3)*

Irenaeus does not simply say that the victory of Christ over sin and death is the foundation of our salvation. He goes further by seeing in the Resurrection the ultimate sign of the constant presence of the Word alongside humans, a presence which goes so far as to include humans in the filial relationship which is His. We are united with the Son. The Resurrection opens the possibility of this new filiation, of this new birth which is nothing other than the birth to incorruptible life. It is by a whole chain of ideas that Irenaeus manages to say that the Son makes himself accessible to all humans and this access to the Son by humans is nothing other than the life of the Risen within them. It is by means of the Resurrection that the Incarnate Word achieves the destruction of sin and makes human beings capable of bearing incorruptible life.

"And His light appeared and made the darkness of the prison disappear, and hallowed our birth and destroyed death, loosing those same fetters in which we were enchained. And He manifested the resurrection, Himself becoming the first-begotten of the dead, and in Himself raising up man that was fallen, lifting him up far above the heaven to the right hand of the glory of the Father." (Dem. 38)

Once more, Irenaeus sends us back to the theme of a recumbent being, lying on the ground, so to speak. For humans to stand up and get nearer to Life, the 'fetters' and the 'darkness' of their sinful condition pinning them to the ground must be transformed into liberation and glory. The Resurrection initiates the new era of the lordship of the Son in opposition to the reign of evil.

The way Irenaeus insists on the Lordship of the Son is surely other than a mere fascination with the image of the victorious Christ. For him, this Lordship is inseparable from the problem of human freedom and our propensity towards sin. This is why Irenaeus often introduces the Lord as the 'just man.' If Christ 'has pre-eminence over all things,' as Irenaeus says, he does so as 'a just and holy man...good, well-pleasing to God, perfect in all ways...' (Dem. 39) This perfection of the Son who has become Lord is much more than morally meaningful. It is theologically meaningful, as it evokes the constant tension between the universal Lordship of the Risen and human freedom. If the project of becoming in the image of God is inscribed in every single human being without exception, it is not imposed as an external imperative. One can see that Irenaeus is troubled by this. *"Why is his goodness, which does not save all (thus), defective?" (A.H. Bk IV, 33: 2)* The question is a terrible one; God's goodness and mercy and the Son's victory over evil do not prevent a certain number of humans from moving away from God. They are not saved *against* their will. The fruit of the Resurrection can be rejected.

It is in *freedom* that Irenaeus finds an answer to this riddle. Because of our freedom, the work of salvation is also ours. It does not stop with Christ's personal victory. This victory leads all humans to commit to the same fight. This is how they gradually become like the perfect Image of the Father who is the Son and who was the first to vanquish evil. They will become 'precious in the eyes of the Father', as Irenaeus says, because they will resemble the Son.

Now for Irenaeus this configuration to become like the Son goes as far as the recreation of human beings. When this configuration has attained the most secret places in the human heart, to the extent of a radical transformation, they will cross over the threshold to a life which bears the gift of incorruptibility. This is where the work of the Holy Spirit is to be understood because the 're-creation of man in the image of the Son' in the Resurrection is consistent with the vocation bestowed on the first human being when he was made in the image of God.

This new birth in incorruptibility is, above all, the work of the Creative Spirit. Let us recall that with Irenaeus creation is something never completed. From the beginning, human life is destined to become incorruptible. The Resurrection which enables humans to receive this gift is thus neither alien nor added on to the creation. It is rather a sign that, in us, the Spirit has done his work well.

Our vocation of being configured to be like that of the Son has finally been achieved at the point when it becomes possible for the Spirit to lift us up to the never-ending life of God.

"Such men as these shall be properly called both 'pure' and 'spiritual' and 'those living to God' because they possess the Spirit of the Father, who purifies man and raises him up to the life of God." (A.H. Bk V, 9: 2)

Let us finish by saying that Irenaeus is totally true to his insight that the Risen Christ is at the heart of human life. Our reconfiguration in the image of God and the Son starts here on earth, but it does not stop here. This process, an integral aspect of each human being, goes on even after death. It becomes even easier after death since sin is no longer an obstacle. Moreover, reconfiguration also includes the body, the incorruptible life of the body after death.

Resurrection is nothing other than the sign and the token of the completion of our vocation to be in the image of God. As for the Spirit, He is responsible for the smooth running, so to speak, of this ongoing creative process. He is the one at work within us so that the fruit of the Resurrection of Christ may be fully efficient in us, in other words, so that the victory of Christ may open the way to our elevation to life in God.

This is a teaching which is in no way original or odd. It is the Apostolic tradition as it has been handed down to the Christians in the second century, and more particularly, to the Christians by their bishop in the Church of Lyon. Is it also a language that can speak to Christians in our century? The images of the Creed have remained unchanged to the present day: 'descent to the dead,' 'on the third day,' and 'resurrection of the flesh.' I think that Irenaeus' approach, if not his language, is highly instructive as it shows us how important it is to go beyond the literal meaning of words in order to arrive at their deeper meaning. It is the symbolic dimension which is at work here, the same as in the sacraments. ■

CHAPTER VI

He Will Come Again to Judge the Living and the Dead

The Gnostics compelled Irenaeus to speak of the ultimate ends: the Resurrection of the dead, the Last Judgment, hell, and the kingdom of the Just. The Gnostics anxiously asked themselves: "Where does evil come from?" The answer they gave to the question was, unfortunately, unacceptable for faith, hence it was unsustainable for believers who sympathized with them. It was the absolute negation of what the Christian faith held essential, that is to say the dialectics between universal *salvation* and human *freedom* capable of refusing it.

The Gnostics had indeed denied both of these assertions of faith by their belief that they were a chosen minority set apart from the mass of people doomed to perdition. From such a viewpoint, according to which only a small handful of predestined humans were to be allowed into the Kingdom of heaven, freedom was pointless (the destiny of all of them being inexorably predetermined).

In order to deter the Christians who were tempted by such ideas, Irenaeus directed them to the Scriptures' teachings about God who does not wish to lose anything of His creation and about the responsibility of humans who are free to accept or reject God's plan for them.

In order to make his point about this twofold assertion, Irenaeus evokes two major eschatological images in the Bible, the Last Judgment, and the accounts of the Apocalypse. We are going to tackle these two points by asking the question of how Irenaeus dealt with the dialectics, *salvation* and *freedom*. Does he provide us with some insights into the mystery of evil and the victory of Christ over it? More precisely, what does Irenaeus say about those who are apparently impervious to God's mercy? How does he view the situation of those who remain faithful to Christ right to the end? In the way he views this faithfulness that can be so severely tested, is there something that echoes the issue as it is expounded today?

The Sad Logic of Hardened Sinners

With Irenaeus, one thing is certain. If humans are sinners, God who created them is not responsible for it.

"The skill of God, therefore, is not defective...but the man who does not obtain it is the cause to himself of his own imperfection." (A.H. Bk IV, 39: 3)

In this we recognize the now familiar theme of growth, but this time it is about an uninterrupted growth. If some people cannot manage to fulfill their vocation to be in the image of God, it is not the Creator's fault. It is not that God made them incapable of receiving this grace. This is the result of their free and conscious choice.

This sad reality, borne out by history and confirmed by God's revelation, raises the question of the ultimate destiny of those who deliberately choose the path of sin. For Irenaeus, to see them fall back into the primeval void from which they were drawn is out of the question, since nothing in this material world is meant to disappear, except the unfinished state which is currently ours.

There is a significant page in *Against Heresies (Bk I, 10: 1)* showing Irenaeus' position on this point. However, let us recall that nothing he says here involves personal speculations. He simply gives us Scriptural teaching. This is the key to his teaching about those definitively installed in the way of sin.

Irenaeus does not make up anything concerning faith, especially when dealing with the sensitive issue of sinners forever separated from God. He recalls how the rebel angels were sent to hell; then he immediately adds that some people, godless, unjust, iniquitous, and blasphemous, share the fate of the corrupt angels and apostates. But, for these sinners it is particularly tragic, as such destiny was never meant to happen to them.

"For, the idea of lost humans runs counter to God's design, in so far as everlasting fire was not made ready for them, but for the one who seduced them and caused them to sin." (A.H. Bk III, 23: 3)

Hell is against human nature in every sense of the word if hell is the dreaded sanction that strikes beings who are freely and obstinately steeped in their rejection of God. "Irenaeus only sees in this an echo of the Scriptures in which the everlasting punishment of hell is never presented, but as the ultimate outcome of evil freely wished for," says Adelin Rousseau, [18] the translator of *Against Heresies*. It is

---

18   Adelin Rousseau, "L'éternité des peines de l'enfer," dans *Nouvelle revue théologique,* November-December 1977, p. 839.

the meaning that Irenaeus gives to the words of Christ who, in the Gospel, speaks to those who will be on his left-hand side at the Last Judgment. If the reprobates suffer the same fate as that of the rebel angels, it is because they willed it. They are those, says Irenaeus, who *"persevere in works of wickedness, without repentance, and without retracing their steps." (A.H. Bk III, 23: 3).*

As we have seen before, the epitome of this persistence in sin is Cain *"but (he) even added sin to sin, indicating his state of mind by his action." (A.H. Bk III, 23: 4)* Irenaeus harks back to the same theme in other contexts, in places where this idea touches the mystery of evil in the human heart hardened in its choice:

"Those who fly from the eternal light of God...are themselves the cause to themselves of their inhabiting eternal darkness, destitute of all good things, having become to themselves the cause of (their con-signment to) an abode of that nature." (A.H. Bk IV, 39: 4)

If the fate of the wicked depends ultimately upon their own will, what about divine judgment? In Irenaeus, it is anything but arbitrary. It is rather the ratification of the choices made in this life. On this subject, above all, Irenaeus refers us to John's idea of Judgment, a judgment between those who led their earthly lives either in blindness or in light, in other words, Christ has not come to condemn but to make a distinction. This comes from his quote from John 3:19, "This is the verdict: Light has come into the world, but people loved darkness instead of light because their deeds were evil." It is clear that Irenaeus is inspired by this view of Judgment, which was not that of a divine condemnation falling pitilessly on the sinner's head but rather the ratification by God of humankind's ultimate will to move away from Him.

"...on as many as, according to their own choice, depart from God, He inflicts that separation from Himself which they have cho-

sen of their own accord. But...separation from light is darkness...God, however, does not punish them immediately of Himself, but that punishment falls upon them because they are destitute of all that is good... It is in this matter just as occurs in the case of a flood of light: those who have blinded themselves, or have been blinded by others, are forever deprived of the enjoyment of light. It is not, (however), that the light has inflicted upon them the penalty of blindness, but it is that the blindness itself has brought calamity upon them." (A.H. Bk V, 27: 2)

In fact, Irenaeus does not let us say much more about the judgment of the wicked, since he remains very close to what is said in the Scriptures. If we ask the question: What will then happen to the reprobates? The answer, says Adelin Rousseau, is very simple: "The biblical texts quoted by Irenaeus do not mention them, neither will Irenaeus. They are beyond the scope of his thinking. Consequently, the most elementary and healthy approach requires that you stop looking for...any kind of clue as to the fate of the reprobates." On the subject of this mystery, he only echoes one of the great assertions of the Scriptures and nothing more. He has a clear preference for everything related to God's tenderness and mercy.

This hesitation on his part to condemn the sinner in a radical way is consistent with his view of evil as a reality which, in part, goes beyond any wickedness of which human beings are capable. The weakness in judgment that Irenaeus attributed to Adam as the cause for his fall implies a frail human freedom. The latter, far from being under the perfect control of an informed and clear conscience, is in part, subject to a greater force, which Irenaeus calls 'Satan.' In this, Irenaeus seems to acknowledge that the tragic dimension of life is not entirely due to sin. In other words, sinful humankind is not totally responsible for a divided creation, crucified by suffering. This viewpoint is essential. We have to go back to this point after considering the second aspect of our topic, namely the Judgment of the righteous.

How are the faithful to take part in the final victory of Christ over death? [19]

The Righteous Justified in Their Hope

The encounter of the righteous with the Lord at the Parousia addresses a subject that we have not yet touched on, namely millenarianism, the thousand-year old Kingdom on earth, distinct from the Kingdom of God. In the Apocalypse of Saint John, chapter 20, the author speaks of Satan in chains and of the reign of the righteous with Christ for a thousand years. The same account appears in the pages of *Against Heresies*, Book V, chapters 25-36. Some of Irenaeus' exegetes, ill at ease with this eschatology, call into question the authenticity of his pages on the subject of millenarianism. And, in fact, Erasmus' edition of *Against Heresies* published in 1526, the first publication after almost a thousand years' silence concerning Irenaeus' work, did not include the descriptions about millenarianism. Maybe they existed originally but had subsequently been suppressed after Origen, Jerome and, above all, Saint Augustine had insisted on the fact that millenarianism was not compatible with faith.

What complicated the issue was the discovery of a Greek manuscript in 1575 in which the descriptions of millenarianism were included in the text of *Against Heresies*. Thereafter, it was impossible to overlook these passages. Some among its critics find them simply grotesque and fanciful. Others, while accepting the genuine character of this eschatology, do not hide their uneasiness.

---

19 See Pierre Grelot. *Le Monde à venir*, Paris, Ed. du centurion, coll. "Croire et comprendre," 1974.

I do not mean to tackle the subject from the point of view of an exegete. It is enough simply to recall two things: on the one hand, comparable descriptions do exist in the Bible even in the Gospel and on the other hand it is likely that Irenaeus simply voiced an eschatological trend recognized by all the churches of his time, this because of the scrupulous care that he always took when passing on what he believed to be the faith of the Apostles.

More important for us here is the meaning that is revealed through Irenaeus' millenarianism. B. Reynders is convinced that Irenaeus' apocalyptic vision is quite simply the logical conclusion of his major theological insights: "All his being and his faith, he says, call for this universal restoration." [20] In this new context of millenarianism, let us clarify this assertion by a few observations concerning the identity of Christ, the contingent character of creation and recapitulation.

The Identity of Christ

The Risen lives in the same flesh, which was His, during his stay on earth. The identity of Christ requires that his earthly body and his glorious body be the same. Consequently, once risen, humans will also benefit from their own identity in their resuscitated flesh. Whatever their fate, they will remain strictly as they were before their death. Even, if Irenaeus does not dwell on the fate of the wicked, he does continue his thinking about the righteous. If they are raised in the same body, the latter will nonetheless be transformed. This idea provides Irenaeus with an unexpected development about eschatological hope.

---

20 B. Reynders, "Optimisme et théocentrisme chez saint Irénée; dans *Recherches de théologie ancienne et médiévale*, 8 ème année, 1936, p. 225-252.

He introduces the worldly kingdom of the Son during a thousand years (after the resurrection of the righteous) by means of images of a new earth and that of a banquet. It is about a new earth, and not a completely different earth, since God has infinite respect for everything He has created. Nothing is lost. At the end of time, not only will humanity's expectation be fulfilled but also that of the whole creation which *"waiteth for the manifestation of the sons of God." (Rm 8:19; A.H. Bk V, 32: 1)* In this, Irenaeus highlights the continuity of God's plan. It is *His* creation, the same as the one we know, which will be transformed and will be the kingdom of the righteous with His Son.

This also explains the image of the eschatological banquet. If a human still needs a body, *his or her* own body in order to be human, *his or her* incarnate and bodily identity is linked to the need for food. In this, Irenaeus' exegesis is based on the promise made by Jesus to his disciples at the Last Supper when he spoke of the 'new wine' that he was going to drink in the kingdom of His Father (Mt. 26:9). It is clear for him that the righteous will be invited to the Son's banquet, and these, in their own transformed flesh: *"Nor, again, are they who drink it devoid of flesh, for to drink of that which flows from the vine pertains to flesh, and not spirit." (A.H. Bk V, 33: 1)*

The Universal Restoration

The universal restoration mentioned by B. Reynders brings us back to a second observation: the contingent and unfinished character of the created. If everyone is destined for salvation, then historically it is clear that all do not receive the revelation of the love of God, even the best-intentioned. For example, let us take the former Just of Israel born before Jesus. At the Last Judgment and the coming of the kingdom of Christ, they will see fulfilled what had only been, until then, their deepest desire: to be face to face with their Lord. On the day that they see the face of the Word, previously hidden from their sight, they will know for sure that His providence and thoughtful love have always been with them.

But, since the coming of Christ, universal salvation also concerns the Just who have no knowledge of him. Some of the Just will only know Christ at the very end. This will be in his kingdom when the Son puts an end to their ignorance, when he fully reveals the mystery of the Father to all.

The thousand-year reign is an answer to another aspect of finiteness, the unfinished character of humanity and its need of time. If Irenaeus says that the righteous will stay with Christ on earth for a thousand years, and if he thinks that there will be no immediate transfer into the glory of the Father, it is because humans need time to get used to the presence of their Lord, even after the resurrection. Even in their resuscitated state the righteous will need to make progress, that is to say, to be more and more willing to live with the Son and behold Him, an indispensable preparation for living in the glory of God.

The one thousand-year reign is thus presented as the time when the true understanding will be communicated by the Son in a visible and personal way to prepare the righteous for their meeting with the Father. Here we see the difficulty for Irenaeus to conceive how it will be possible for humans immediately to receive after death the overwhelming fullness of glory. He thus thinks that humanity will need more time to prepare for it. In order to see and partake in the glory of God, humans must really be ready:

"The righteous shall reign in the earth, waxing stronger by the sight of the Lord; and through Him they shall become accustomed to partake in the glory of God the Father." (A.H. Bk V, 35: 1) Further on,

Irenaeus insists on the same idea, *"And as he (man) rises actually, so also shall he be actually disciplined beforehand for incorruption and shall go forwards and flourish in the times of the kingdom, in order that he may be capable of receiving the glory of the Father." (A.H. Bk V, 35: 2)*

Apparently, Irenaeus thinks that this world, our present life, is not enough to prepare ourselves for the boundless happiness awaiting us. The Son needs to be more directly involved in our final training, so to speak. It will be a thousand times easier, he thinks, as we shall no longer be distracted by the worries and temptations of our present life.

This recapitulation is quite consistent with Irenaeus' idea that communion with God is a reality in the making. It is also linked to the similar theme of divine teaching skills. Humans will need it even after their death. If the thousand-year kingdom is to be treated as a teaching tool to enable humanity to receive the glory of the Father, it is because the risen are not ghosts. They will not experience the vision of God bereft of their flesh, but in and through it. They will behold the Father's face still in their condition of incarnate spirits. The flesh thus prepared is necessary for the righteous. They must gradually adjust in order to see and partake in the glory of God. The kingdom of the Son at the end of time will quite efficiently prepare the way for this adjustment.

Recapitulation

A third observation concerns the universal restoration at the end of time: recapitulation. Let us recall that *recapitulation* means to bring all humans together, from the first to the last, under one single Head, Christ. The judgment complies with the need to make visible the Lord's act of recapitulation and somehow the need to justify the choice made by the righteous to dwell in the shadow under His wings, despite the temptations in this life to deny His caring and loving presence. By the final recapitulation in which all will be gathered together before the Lord, Irenaeus seeks to reassure the Christians of his time about the fact that their sufferings are not in vain. Because they shared Christ's sufferings during their earthly lives, they will see their hardship recapitulated and transformed by the One in Whom they have not lost hope. It is just and right that the disciple should share the joy of *Christus Victor* in His kingdom. It is a simple question of justice. Sooner or later his fidelity must be acknowledged. In spite of appearances, Eschaton, the outburst of the divine, the presence of the divine in history, must be recognized as being at work in their lives.

This way of seeing things shows the complex character of hope in Irenaeus. The three themes that we have just seen, Christ's identity, the unfinished state of the created, and recapitulation seen from the eschatological point of view of millenarianism, constitute a hope which holds together terrestrial and celestial realities. It is a hope that acknowledges the fact that the promise made by God has, from now on, actual substance and that God is always at work in the lives of people. At the same time, the image of the ultimate ends, especially those of the thousand-year reign, places hope within the unfinished dimension of salvation. It is an image telling us that life is not totally in the grip of temporal and positivist history.

If I insist here on the word *image*, it is deliberate. We now know that there is no representation capable of adequately touching the essence of our hope. It is not important for us to know whether Irenaeus believed the thousand-year reign to be an exact description of future reality. What we need to remember here is the overall direction pointed out by this image, that is to say, that the last and final events have no finish line. In its own way Irenaeus' eschatology says that there is a disproportion between humanity's historical progress and its true progress which escapes all definition. An endless process of fulfillment cannot be simplified to a precise ending. We shall have the opportunity to come back to this idea when dealing with the last article of the Creed, eternal life.

But now, let us get back to the question left open at the beginning of this chapter about the forces of evil which, in Irenaeus, go beyond the frailty, the tragic character of human life. As we have just seen, the Last Judgment in Irenaeus well shows the human condition as it is, finite by nature.

On the one hand, there is something unresolved in the fact that Irenaeus lets the wicked slip out of his focus without saying more; on the other hand, there is something inconclusive about the way that he sees the righteous progressively discover the meaning of their faithfulness in the Kingdom of the Son.

Human Freedom and the Tragic Dimension of Life

What follows is about humans overwhelmed by a force which strikes them down, but which they cannot, if they are believers, attribute to God. In this, Irenaeus makes it possible for us to think through the tragic dimension of human life, without reducing it to sin alone. In this way he touches on questions that we ask ourselves today after Auschwitz.

What comes out is the idea of human freedom as being deeply marked by contingency. Because of its finite nature, it is by itself incapable of engendering evil in the absolute. What is inexplicable and tragic is the occasional unhinged magnitude of consequences resulting from its choices, a sort of exponential growth of evil arising from a single point in the beginning, that of the personal act of the sinner. In short, human freedom is shown to be overwhelmed by a force greater than itself. Irenaeus gives this force the name of 'Satan' or 'Fallen Angel.' Does this partly exonerate humans from the consequences of their freedom?

Ultimately, humans are not totally responsible for the horrors of this world. Thus, their sin is not a totally adequate explanation for evil. The mystery as to the ultimate origin of evil remains intact.

An image of God comes out of this way of seeing things. An image which does not easily fit in the classic (rather deistic) categories of God the creator as a transcendent God, totally set apart from humanity by the ineffable perfection of His attributes. One who would not be close to humans except through His Son offered in sacrifice on the Cross.

In fact, God the creator is also close to humanity. If this world is really *His* world, as Irenaeus says, the consequence is that He cannot be indifferent to humans in this world, with all the commitment that this implies for Him. The human condition is *His* business and not only that of His Son!

Such a way of putting human sin into perspective has consequences for eschatology. It no longer appears as a discourse about God confined by the narrow limits of legal proceedings relegated to the end of time. From this viewpoint, eschatology is already at work in this world in the sense that it is the presence of God committing Himself in full view of all on the side of the righteous as guarantor of their ultimate defense.

Of course, this answer sometimes meets fierce resistance from people wounded by their impotence in the face of evil, since here we are dealing with eschatological judgment. Nowadays it has provoked much criticism from those who blame religion for being a kind of anesthesia because the innocent who suffer would only have to wait for the Last Judgment to be rehabilitated. We know that this objection is not groundless, but for the Christian it is contradicted and challenged by the Beatitudes.

As far as we are concerned here, Irenaeus stresses the importance of the biblical image of eschatological judgment not only because it corresponds to one of the great themes in the early church, but also because of the mystery of evil. If God is just, the fidelity of his servants must be acknowledged, but one must admit that in history a countless number of innocent victims will never be acknowledged. Never in this world will they find solace and justification for enduring, consciously or not, Christ's sufferings in their bodies and minds.

This is the tragic dimension of evil. One must admit that it is impossible to scale it down to mere humans' wrongdoing or to suggest that it could gradually be eradicated with a little more effort. There is something demonic, implacable, in woes that afflict people, which is disproportionate to their mistakes or sins.

Confronted by this mystery, Irenaeus insists on eschatology since it is unthinkable that the name of the righteous should be forgotten forever. This would be a monstrous injustice.

Yet again, the Last Judgment is still present in our century in the sense that it remains in the heart of the righteous as a promise and a hope that they might see the total eradication of evil one day.

Is this an easy way to rationalize the issue? Or rather, is it a concession to our need to see that debts are paid? These are not trivial accusations. And yet, the problem is that making such accusations plunges us back into the horror of the absurd where there is no justice for the innocent since there is no judge. For Irenaeus who wrote after the persecutions in 177, as for the theologians thinking through the abomination of Auschwitz today, this absurdity cannot be accepted for one simple reason, faith in the Gospel. In this too, a certain degree of freedom remains, that of accepting – or not – the message of hope of the Gospel that bears witness to an ultimate justice.

When speaking of justice in terms that evoke the relationship between creation and incarnation in Irenaeus, Marie Dominique Chenu says the following:

"Incarnation is in line with creation...Incarnation is the way that creation is fulfilled... Thus, when we say that a testimony will be a testimony of justice, which justice are we talking about? It is the law according to which the reality of the world is being constructed by man. If man does not abide by the laws of balance and equity, he disturbs the world and brings disruption into creation... In other words, justice does not first depend on morals but on the metaphysics of creation. Thus justice seems to be the permanent rule for the construction of the world. It is when I bear witness to justice that God is made manifest. [21]

It is along these guidelines that the necessity appears today to bear witness to the Last Judgment, and to the justice that will be revealed in the restored creation and the risen bodies of the righteous. ■

---

21 Marie-Dominique Chenu, in *Spiritus*, no. 49, p. 139.

CHAPTER VII

I Believe in the Holy Spirit

The Identity of the Holy Spirit in Irenaeus

At the end of the second century, Trinitarian theology had not yet become highly complex and had not yet given rise to subsequent theological dispute. Like the church of his time, the bishop of Lyon only refers to the work and the gifts of the Holy Spirit without clarifying Its ultimate reality. In this respect, he is very faithful to the biblical revelation which refers to the Spirit of God without insisting on Its identity as a divine subject distinct from the Father and the Son. Irenaeus does not speak of the Spirit in a way that would make us think of the subsequent definitions of the Trinity. In him, there is still the same imprecision of vocabulary as is found in the Bible: the Spirit of God, the Lord is Spirit... (See 2 Co 3: 17 and A.H. Bk III, 10: 3)

In other words, though it is quite legitimate to speak of the Father, the Son and the Spirit in Irenaeus, as in the Bible, no clearly enunciated formal doctrine about the Holy Spirit is to be found in his writing. He asserts the divinity of the Holy Spirit, without seeking to know whether Its origin is different from that of the Son. For Irenaeus, the important thing is to assert that both are the Offspring of the Father and His Hands. According to J. Mambrino, [22] Irenaeus says, *"The Father did not need any angels, that is to say alien to or other than Himself, in order to create the world and man, because He had His Offspring, the Son and the Spirit, also respectively called the Word and Wisdom." (See A.H. Bk IV, 20: 1).*

As for the Son, the Spirit derives from the Father as opposed to created things, which were brought forth from nothingness by the creative act of the Father. By insisting on the very term *Offspring* in order to express the origin of the Son and of the Holy Spirit, Irenaeus does not mean to express what distinguishes one from the other – but what their common transcendence is – as opposed to the origin of all living things. On the whole, as is said in Proverbs 8:25, Wisdom – identified by Irenaeus with the Holy Spirit – was 'given birth' by God. *"Wisdom…which is the Spirit, was present with Him, (the Father) anterior to all creation… The Lord created me the beginning of His ways in His work: He set me up from everlasting, in the beginning, before He made the earth, before He established the depths…" (A.H. Bk IV, 20: 3; see Pr 8:22-25).*

How The Holy Spirit Relates to Humanity

The anthropological dimension of the issue

The Gnostics compelled Irenaeus to answer the question, how can one become 'spiritual' if one is linked to a body, if the body is to be considered as an essential part of human finality? To answer this question, Irenaeus gave great importance to human corporeality. Human beings are *for* God not only because they are incarnate spirits, but also because they are human. In fact, human beings will

---

22 J. Mambrino: "Les deux mains de Dieu dans l'oeuvre de saint Irénée," *Nouvelle revue théologique*, n° 78, 1957, p. 355-370.

be perfectly in the likeness of their creator when they have reached full maturity, becoming incarnate spirits who are 'living humans' in the full sense of the words 'humans fully alive.' But, what is the *spirit* of human beings...the non-sentient part of a human?

We have already rejected in Irenaeus' thinking the classical notion of the *soul* as having a life of its own, independent of the body. For him, as for the Bible, the link is so intimate between body and soul that the body is nothing other than the exterior expression of the soul. In this respect, his view is close to our modern conception, which is prone to consider a human being as a whole (a psychosomatic view). It is harder for us to understand the meaning of the third term of biblical and Irenaean anthropology, the Spirit.

The linguistic equivalents – *pneuma* in Greek and *esprit* in French, do not succeed in expressing all the nuances of the Hebrew word *rûah*, the divine breath that animates human beings without being of them. (See earlier in chapter two) The biblical mindset, which is that of Irenaeus, makes a distinction between the soul that animates humans and the source of their lives. On the contrary, the Greek mindset identified the soul with the spirit of which it was some kind of emanation, whereas biblical thinking made a distinction between the soul and the living source, God himself. *Rûah*, or the Spirit, thus comes from God. It is within humans without being identified with them. Even more importantly, *it is that by which we are able to receive the Holy Spirit in ourselves.*

This is where things become more complicated since Irenaeus uses the word 'spirit' with some ambiguity in his writings. The publishers of *Sources Chrétiennes* have tried to make things easier by using a capital letter when they are fairly sure that it deals with the Divine Spirit. But, even when it is quite clear that it refers to the divine principle in humanity, one question remains. Is this principle totally extrinsic to humans and unnecessary to their integrity or to their natural perfection?

Our difficulty when reading Irenaeus is that he refers to human beings as totally tripartite (body – soul – spirit). They live *by* the Spirit as a result of *being alive*. Without the participation of their spirit in the Spirit of God, they would not even exist. In other words, humans live naturally, if I may say so, *by* the Holy Spirit, and this independently of all moral consideration. The participation of human life in the life of the Holy Spirit is an anthropological question before it is a question for morals or for a theology of grace. All humans, are alive quite simply because of their participation in the life of God, that is to say, the Spirit, and this whether they are good or not. For this reason, to keep the word *gift* only for the sanctifying life of the Spirit, separately from the divine force that naturally animates humanity, may lead to confusion.

It is true that at times Irenaeus himself suggests this distinction (*See A.H. Bk V, 1: 3 and Bk V, 12: 2*). In these passages, he seems to make a distinction between the breath of life, which makes human beings human, and the vivifying Spirit that makes them perfect in the moral sense. And indeed, some exegetes did not hesitate to give a 'supernaturalist' reading of these texts. Is this the way Irenaeus thought? Is this his anthropology?

The trickiest point is to know the nature of this force which animates humans. Is it about two different life principles? It could well be the case. The phrase 'two principles' is not to be discarded, provided that one remains faithful to Irenaeus' fundamental intuition; it is not about two lives which are different in nature, but about one and the same person willing, or not, to live by the Spirit which animates him or her.

In order to understand this teaching, one would need to put the issue of the Spirit, by which humans are alive, back into the essential context of growth. What makes the difference between people is not whether the Spirit is within them or not, but the quality, the degree to which the Spirit is at work in their lives. Instead of referring to a state of grace due to the presence of the Holy Spirit, one must stress the idea that all live by the Spirit, but some more enthusiastically than others.

Starting from an initial frail state, human beings do, or do not, make progress in what they are, namely beings whose life principle has been the Spirit from the beginning and forever. Irenaeus' anthropology goes thus far. One can assert this, even though the inherent link between the human spirit and the Divine Spirit is not sufficiently made clear in his writings to meet our requirement for absolute consistency. His theology of the Spirit is, in many respects, as in the Scriptures, spontaneous and not fully worked-out. What is important for humans is to live in a way that is consistent with the life principle that animates them. To reject this is to contradict their own logic, their own consistency as the image of God already in this world, called upon to be more and more in His likeness. For this reason, it can be said that sanctification is essentially a process of humanization. This is what we are going to see now.

Growth, The Work of the Spirit

If we follow Irenaeus' logic, sin is something that affects humanity in its entirety and not only the spiritual part of its being. This is also true for sanctification. To live in harmony with the Spirit within us is to live in accordance with our deepest and most authentic being, hence its beneficial effects even for our body. To become a saint is to be sanctified in one's whole being: *"For by the hands of the*

Father, that is, by the Son and the Holy Spirit, man, and not (merely) a part of man, was made in the likeness of God." (A.H. Bk V, 6: 1)

Just like the Word, the Spirit makes humans 'alive.' Right from the beginning, the Spirit takes possession of humans in order to work on them, to prepare them for the incorruptibility that will transfigure their whole being. This is exactly what Irenaeus' meditation on the flesh possessed by the Spirit means in chapter V. The flesh does not possess the Spirit, but the former is possessed by the latter.

"What, again, are the possessions of the deceased? The various parts of the man, surely, which rot in the earth. But these are inherited by the Spirit when they are translated into the kingdom of heaven... For he who lives inherits, but the flesh is inherited." (A.H. Bk V, 9: 4)

This thought leads Irenaeus to think of the beautiful Pauline image about the wild olive tree and the cultivated olive tree (Rm 11:16-24). With the image of the graft, Irenaeus compares those who prefer to remain as 'a wild olive tree' to those who prefer to become a 'fruit-bearing olive tree' thanks to their accepting the graft of life. Humans accept to be 'grafted in' by the Spirit, or rather the Spirit is grafted into them. When they receive the fruit-bearing olive tree of the Spirit, they become able to bear the fruit of the works of the just. Otherwise, they bear wild fruit, sterile in justice (*see A.H. Bk V, 10: 1*). In fact, humans who do not live by the Spirit are unfruitful like trees bearing no more. They are, somehow, already dead, 'not having life' (*A.H. Bk V, 9: 3*) even though they go on breathing, walking and eating.

As for those who welcome the fruit-bearing olive tree of the Spirit, they become 'alive for God'; they have been brought up into 'living to God' (*A.H. Bk V, 9: 2*). The dynamics of the Spirit makes them gradually ripen so that, in the end, they may enjoy the incorruptibility of life without end. This idea deserves to be stressed as it calls into question a certain moralizing conception of holiness which can be called 'exemplariness.' In Irenaeus, the gradual sanctification of humanity is much more than the simple external reproduction of the model. It is not about an imitation that would remain superficial. Thanks to the Spirit, humans are illuminated from within. In a word, the Spirit is Itself, the internalization of the image after which humanity was created, the Son.

This assertion sends us back to the need to specify in what way the Spirit works towards the sanctification of humans. Let us recall that Irenaeus has no specific theology of the Holy Spirit. He does not give, as the Church was to do later, a specific role to the Spirit when dealing with sanctification. With him, it is better to speak of the 'pneumatic' action of the Father and of the Son. The basic idea is that the Living God makes humans alive with His own Life, the Spirit. Totally inaccessible as such, He reveals Himself to them as Spirit. It is during this process that the word 'Spirit comes in to express the revelation of the coming together of God with the ineffable human reality. The Spirit expresses this so that humans understand that the One and unique divine Reality is revealed within themselves. Now for Irenaeus, because what is unique in *pneuma* is life, such phrases as 'the Spirit of God' or 'the Spirit of Christ' mean that both the Father and the Son, are revealed to humans as Life and as Spirit. The presence and the action of the Spirit are presented as the way to be human, to be the image of God. The sanctification of humans, by means of the divine action named three times, is the beginning of their participation in the glory of the Uncreated:

"By this arrangement, therefore, and these harmonies, and a sequence of this nature, man, a created and organized being, is rendered after the image and likeness of the uncreated God, the Father planning everything well and giving His commands, the Son carrying

these into execution and performing the work of creating, and the Spirit nourishing and increasing (what is made), but man making progress day by day, and ascending towards the perfect, that is, approximating to the uncreated One." (A.H. Bk IV, 38:3)

In this, once again, perfection is not reduced to its moral dimension, to the appearance of good behavior, or to spiritual exercises for improvement. It is the absorption of all human weaknesses by the strength of the Spirit, *"the weakness of the flesh will be absorbed by the strength of the Spirit."(A.H. Bk V, 9: 2)* The attainment of righteousness and of holiness under the control of the Spirit involves humanity as a whole progressing towards God in this world. This is why the Spirit does not require humans to break away from this world in their progress towards God. On the contrary, the justice of the Spirit is attained within this world, because God *"made the things of time for man, so that coming to maturity in them, he may produce the fruit of immortality; and who, through His kindness, also bestows (upon him) eternal things." (A.H. Bk IV, 5: 1)*

The maturity of humans is not achieved at the expense of, but by means of their humanity. Their corporeal existence in this world is the place for their justification and sanctification. ∎

CHAPTER VIII

I Believe in the Holy Catholic Church and the Communion of Saints

I bring these two assertions together in a single chapter because of Irenaeus' view. The coherence of his vision requires that the communion of saints be part of the Church. I hope my comments on the issue will not only show the truth, but also and above all, the importance of this conception of the Church.

The Church in Lyon, Smyrna, Rome...

We are dealing with the second half of the second century AD. It was the century of the *Pax Romana* when myriads of people living under the authority of Rome safely moved about due to the more or less visible Roman army present everywhere. For the Church it was a kind of 'Spring' in spite of outbreaks of persecution here and there. It was spring because of the numerous conversions in all strata of the population. It was also the case because of the theological insights springing forth in the writings of thinkers like Irenaeus and Justin preparing the Golden Age of the Church Fathers.

This period of peace and stability greatly contributed to the development of the Church everywhere in the Empire. We have the testimony of Pliny the Younger, governor of Bithynia on the shore of the Black Sea. His letter to the emperor Trajan in the year 110, asking for instructions concerning a trial against Christians, is evidence for the existence of the Church in this remote area.

Although the Church was beginning to make its presence felt all over, one must point out that this was principally in the cities because Christianity in the early centuries was essentially an urban phenomenon, a Church for townsfolk united around their bishop. The means of conversion par excellence, of establishment and promulgation of Christianity in the Roman Empire, was the local community governed by its bishop.

The second-century Church was both missionary and active in the cities. In each city, a single bishop presided over a single Church to which belonged all those who proclaimed the faith of the Apostles. All Christians in the same town were part of the same local community with its officials, its regular meetings, its common-good fund contributed to by its members, its charities for the poor, the sick, and the socially abandoned.

In a city, there was only one *ecclesia*, a single community presided over by a *presbyterium* and its bishop, all around the same Eucharistic table. This unity was considered by the second-century Church as one of its greatest assets. It is true that Christians still used to meet in small groups in people's homes, but the ideal was still there. In the same city, they all gathered together around the same table, proclaiming the same faith with one voice. This is why Irenaeus, in his writings, did not refer to the Church of Lyon or Rome, but to the Church *in* Lyon, *in* Rome and to the Church that *lived in* the city of Lyon. It was always one and the same Church being in a particular place with everything that was needed to be a Church.

We have already seen that this unity was still frail in the second century. The Church was threatened by two kinds of danger, schism and heresy. The heretics were people more or less initiated in Christian doctrines, but they were not necessarily baptized. The great heretics were strong personalities who surrounded themselves with disciples and launched truly seductive campaigns amongst the Baptized with a view to convincing them of the truth of their own teaching in defiance of that of the Church. Round about 150 A.D. there was hardly a local Church that was not disturbed or divided by heresy. It seems that Gnostic sects were made up of groups particularly widespread in the Rhône Valley, hence Irenaeus' efforts. Like other Christians, bishops as well as educated lay people, he sought to fight against the Gnostic heresies which threatened to split up the Baptized and weaken the communities.

These communities were linked with one another, from one city to another. We have evidence in the "letter" sent by the Christians of Lyon and Vienna to the Christians of Asia Minor (today's Turkey) to tell of the courage of their martyrs during the persecution in 177. This letter shows that the Churches were in communion and that throughout the Empire Christians were used to communicating and offering one another mutual support.

Thus, Irenaeus was the bishop of Lyon, the second after Pothinus who died in prison as a result of the ill-treatment he endured during the persecution in 177. From his writings, one can see what kind of bishop Irenaeus was. The few letters and work transmitted to us clearly show that he took his pastoral duty in Lyon very seriously, not only with the Christians from the great capitals of the Empire, but also with the Gauls. It is not surprising since Asians like himself were renowned as being generous and open-minded. How did he see his role as an official of the Church? In what way did this man, who presided over one of the most active and dynamic Churches in the second century, believe in the Church and the communion of saints?

The People in Charge of the Church According to Irenaeus

The Bishop

Irenaeus presents the Church as the community of faith gathered around its bishop and its *presbyterium.* The presbyters are elders of the community and not 'priests' in the modern sense of the word with all that this implies legally. [23]

It is still too close to the beginnings of the Church to speak of a triple hierarchy [bishop, priest, deacon] in the modern sense of the word.

In his book, The Bishop of Rome, P. Tillard said that:

"...we have no serious evidence that there was a bishop in Rome, and not a college of presbyters or episcopes, before the middle of the second century. It is even difficult to prove convincingly that one of the twelve Apostles was at the head of a local church. Only much later on were the twelve (Apostles])considered as 'bishops' of

---

23   Irenaeus refers to 'presbyters,' but one should not equate them with priests as we know them. The 'presbyter' is an elder, a mature, even old man, with a long-term concern for the Church and bearing witness to this by his life and his writings. It is not even clear that he was in charge of an Episcopal task. When Irenaeus speaks of presbyters, one feels that he refers to great witnesses of the faith, maybe bishops (like Papias, the bishop of Hierapolis in Phrygia, for example, who was a disciple of Saint John and according to Irenaeus, a companion of Polycarpus). Irenaeus does not speak of priests. Neither does he say anything of deacons, with the exception of the letter from the Church in Lyon about the martyrs, which mentions Sanctus, the deacon of Vienna.

the first Christian centers. In fact, Irenaeus knew nothing about Peter's episcopate in Rome. He was careful to specify that Linus was the first bishop after the founders, Peter and Paul.[24]

This is the well-advised opinion of a contemporary theologian. And, this is in keeping with what is suggested in Irenaeus' writings. The bishop beginning to appear from the body of presbyters is, first of all, a minister in charge of the fundamental functions of the Church, which are to maintain the link between the faith of the Apostles and that of the Christians who proclaim it, to ensure the unity of the Church gathered at a specific place and time, and to maintain communion among the local Churches. Undoubtedly the 'episcope,' or the bishop that Irenaeus was, in his life and his writings, highlights the importance of the three main functions to be fulfilled by the entire ecclesia and, above all, by its bishop.

One of the great functions of the Church and especially of the bishop is thus to maintain intact the Apostolic tradition, the faith preached and witnessed by the Apostles. As a bishop, Irenaeus feels compelled to champion the truth of the Apostles' faith confronted by heretical teachings. If Christ has given the Church the task of maintaining and transmitting this faith intact, in continuity with its apostolic sources, the bishop is the one who must take on this responsibility.

The 'Succession' of the Bishops

In fact, this continuity of faith, thanks to the bishops, is so fundamental that their succession one after the other, in a local Church, is already a sign of continuity. It is what we call the 'succession of the bishops,' a small phrase of Irenaeus' which has been

---

24 P. Tillard, *L'Evêque de Rome*, Paris, Ed. du Cerf, 1982, p. 111.

much written about throughout the centuries and which deserves to be put correctly into its historical context. Otherwise, we run the risk of attributing to Irenaeus ideas quite contrary to those that he had about the bishop.

Irenaeus was led to speak about the 'succession of the bishops' in order to refute 'Marcionism,' one of the most threatening heresies for the unity of the Church. Marcionites denied the Scriptures and put their faith in a sort of 'secret tradition' handed down not by a visible succession of bishops, but by masters to their disciples. In this, Irenaeus saw a danger to the faith. Faith is not a teaching reserved for an elite; it is not to be transmitted in an occult manner. The Gospel is for all; the bishop is not a spiritual master who teaches his own doctrine. The doctrine, of which he is the guarantor, is a tradition going back to the Apostles, the witnesses who are the founders of our faith in Jesus Christ. This is why those who proclaim this faith are known, not by the name of a spiritual master (as Marcionites, Valentinians, Nicolaitans, etc.) but by the name of 'Christians.'

The phrase 'succession of the bishops' directs Christians back to Christ and not to any spiritual master. Hierarchy is decided according to the mission and the apostolic testimony. Undoubtedly, Irenaeus views the role of the bishop as being part of the apostolic function. This is why the great cities of the Church are not places established by the life of Jesus on this earth (Jerusalem, Bethlehem, Nazareth…) but are points on the map of the world where the Gospel took root thanks to the power of the Spirit spreading out from there to all nations.

It is the testimony of the apostles sent to these places which makes them 'apostolic.' Ephesus, Antioch, Corinth, Rome, etc. – all these cities where an apostle founded a Church are considered as places of the apostolic Church. This is extremely important to understand Irenaeus' stance with respect to the twofold issue for us: the place of the Church in Rome with regards to other Churches, and the Pope as a successor to Peter. In the light of Irenaean thinking, which is often misunderstood on this point but is greatly enlightening when one takes the time to understand it, this issue deserves closer examination.

The Church in Rome

Irenaeus asserts the outstanding apostolic dimension of the local Church in Rome, hence its eminent authority. First he asserts the apostolic tradition of the whole Church, of the Church present everywhere in the world: *"The tradition of the apostles manifested throughout the whole world; and we are in a position to reckon up those who were by the apostles instituted bishops in the Churches, and (to demonstrate) the succession of these men to our own times; those who neither taught nor knew of anything like what these (heretics) rave about,"* (A.H. Bk III, 3: 1), especially the Marcionites.

Two things are to be noted here, the distinction that is made between apostles and bishops, and the fact that the teaching of the bishop is anything but the 'ravings' of the heretics. The apostles instituted bishops in the Churches, but not as their own successors. Irenaeus speaks here of the succession of the *bishops* and not a succession of the apostles because the 'apostle' in the early Church was considered as an ambassador of the Risen Christ, his witness, who belonged to the group on which the Church was founded.

This being said, how does he see the city of Rome in its relation to the other apostolic cities? The way in which he proceeds is very revealing:

"Since, however, it would be very tedious, in such a volume as this, to reckon up the successions of all the Churches...we do this, I

say, by indicating that tradition derived from the apostles, of the very great, the very ancient, and universally known Church founded and organized at Rome by the two most glorious apostles, Peter and Paul; as also (by pointing out) the faith preached to men, which comes down to our time by means of the successions of the bishops. For it is a matter of necessity that every Church should agree with this Church, on account of its preeminent authority, that is, the faithful everywhere, inasmuch as the tradition has been preserved continuously by those (faithful men) who exist everywhere.

The blessed apostles, then, having founded and built up the Church, committed into the hands of Linus the office of the episcopate. Of this Linus, Paul makes mention in the Epistles to Timothy. To him succeeded Anacletus; and after him, in the third place from the apostles, Clement was allotted the bishopric (A.H. Bk III, 3: 2-3).

It is obvious that the local Church of Rome derives its greatness from its particular place and its special link with the 'very glorious apostles Peter and Paul.' If Rome has preeminent origin in comparison to the other Churches, it is due to the fact that it was founded by not just one but two apostles – and what apostles!

Moreover, if Irenaeus refers to Peter and Paul as 'very glorious,' it can only be because of their martyrdom in Rome. For Irenaeus, the death of Peter and Paul in Rome shows that the Church in Rome was stamped by the seal of the greatest apostolic authenticity. Their martyrdom gives Rome the title of 'holy city,' not only the martyrdom of Peter and Paul, but of all the others who suffered there as well. In a letter written to the Corinthians around 95 AD, Clement of Rome tells of an 'immense crowd of the chosen who because of jealousy (the hatred of the heathen) suffered many insults and tortures,' and this was a letter that Irenaeus knew.

For having been the place of both the teaching and martyrdom of Peter and Paul, the local Church of Rome has thus a special and indisputable authority when dealing with faith going back to the apostolic testimony. But, let us be careful to note that the authority that Peter and Paul confer upon this local Church is inseparably linked to their martyrdom and their being major apostles. Why is such importance given to martyrdom? It derives from the fact that it represents the supreme criterion of Christian authenticity. Martyrdom is the absolute seal of evangelical witness. Through death, the witness of faith enters into communion with the glory of Jesus Christ, having somehow gone through the experience of the Cross as Jesus did. We shall come back to this point because, by death, the martyr plays a central role in what we call the 'communion of the saints.'

Thus, we see why Irenaeus says that the Church in Rome has preeminent origin and why he finds it quite logical that the whole Church agrees with it. Peter and Paul, because of their testimony of the evangelical Word rooted in martyrdom, gave the Church in Rome a foundation of exceptional quality. Moreover, in the mindset of the early centuries, the presence of their tombs in Rome makes their belonging to the community in Rome permanent. Rome is thus the seat of Peter and Paul. What can be said about the bishop, Linus, to whom the apostles gave the responsibility of the bishopric? He is what Irenaeus says: *the first bishop* after the founders, Peter and Paul. In no way can it be said that Peter (or Paul) was the first bishop – or even that he was a bishop.

To consider Peter as the first link in a chain of bishops, in a purely legal vision of the transmission of power, is to misrepresent his role. As for Linus, if he is truly the first bishop, he takes his place within the college of bishops as leader of the Church in Rome, *épis-*

copè, he who must safeguard the fidelity to the apostles' faith. Linus' successors, being bishops of the 'preeminent' Church of Rome, are all considered as 'first among the bishops.' The measure of authority of the local Church in Rome is the measure of faith rather than that of power; it is the measure of exemplary testimony rather than that of legality. The Church in Rome is the one that 'recalls' the great and glorious profession of the apostolic faith, where it took place, and where it is preserved.

Later on, as we well know, idiosyncrasies and confrontation between Churches were to lead the Church in Rome to declare itself referee and judge, to claim for itself greater and greater legal power. But, this would require another chapter for historians to deal with.

For Irenaeus, the primacy of the bishop of Rome is not a legal one, it derives from his Church whose origin is in the testimony of Peter and Paul. The bishop of Rome has authority only because of the prerogative of his local Church. From this point of view, Peter's profession of faith and the words that Jesus spoke to him (Mt 16; 13-20) are not really crucial to establish the primacy of the bishops of Rome. This assertion is validated by what Tillard says:

"It has been noticed how the primacy of the local Church of Rome over its bishop, after the apostles' martyrdom, reflects the attitudes of the time. In Greek patriotism, the stress is on the city, not on its officials, however revered they might be. Likewise...from the outset the Church arises from the fraternal communion which makes it 'one in Christ' not by means of he who presides over this communion. Thus, one understands why, during the first centuries, even in Rome, important decisions were made in councils."

It seems to me that this is of prime importance to emphasize what the early Church always practiced: a communion with the bishop of Rome, not as a 'delegate' from the universal Church or as a universal delegate but as a head of the Episcopal college.

The primacy of the bishop of Rome clearly appears as an Episcopal office to be exercised within the communion of the Churches and of the college of bishops. In short, the primacy of the bishop of Rome does not set him apart from the common episcopate. First of all, it functions as a landmark, a memorial of the apostolic faith particular to the Church of Rome. It has a function of care which is first and foremost prophetic. With this, we are in a position to better understand Irenaeus' view, which has often been distorted throughout the centuries, especially from the seventh century onwards when the stakes were to reinforce the power of the pope.

Unfortunately, *Lumen Gentium*, the dogmatic Constitution on the Church of Vatican II, adopted as its own a wrong interpretation of Irenaeus' thinking. According to *Lumen Genium*, Saint Irenaeus testifies:

"Through those who were appointed bishops by the apostles, and through their successors down in our own time, the apostolic tradition is manifested and preserved...the office granted individually to Peter, the first among the apostles, is permanent and is to be transmitted to his successors... Therefore, the Sacred Council teaches that bishops by divine institution have succeeded to the place of the apostles." (Lumen Gentium 1:20)

This is not quite what Irenaeus says, as we have just seen. Nowhere does Irenaeus say that the succession of the bishops is a divine institution. The implied idea too, in *Lumen Gentium*, that Rome would be the origin of the other Churches is in no way in keeping with Irenaeus' ideas. The origin of the Church is to be found in its apostolic foundation in Christ. Rome is something else, something so remarkable in its twofold apostolic origin that it becomes unthinkable for the Church to think of itself as a Church without Rome. In short, the stronger origin of Rome makes it the model of the Church, of the succession of the bishops, in which always and everywhere the apostolic tradition is preserved.

The Communion of Saints

In Irenaeus, the phrase 'communion of saints' does not refer to a specific teaching, but to a context or an atmosphere which pervades everything he says about the Church. From the bishop to the martyr, from the righteous of the first Covenant to the righteous of the Kingdom of the Son, there exists a deep communion of faith, hope and charity. In order to justify this assertion, one would need to quote examples from almost every page of his work. This is why I will only tackle the question from the point of view of charity which creates bonds between the members of Christ. It is in this spirit that I put forward a three-fold development: the righteous with emphasis on martyrdom which is the supreme example of charity, the bishop's holiness, and the holiness of the Church.

The holiness that Irenaeus speaks of has nothing to do with an individualistic piety. Rather, it is a dimension of the Church to which all the members of Christ belong, thanks to the Spirit responsible for the communion and charity among them. This is Irenaeus' ideal, and it is in these terms that one must speak of the communion of saints.

The Righteous and Martyrdom

With good reason, the phrase 'the righteous' evokes for us 'holiness.' Is this also true with the word *righteousness*? Probably not. When Irenaeus says that God will resuscitate *"our mortal bodies which preserved righteousness"* (A.H., *Bk II, 29: 2*), one may spontaneously think of righteousness in the narrow sense of the word, rather than holiness. To Irenaeus, 'preserve righteousness' means, above all, to be faithful to one's creation as the image and likeness of God. But, we must not get it wrong here. We are not dealing with an individualistic type of religion in which the believer is involved in a spiritual struggle to keep intact the image of God that one is, nor a struggle to maintain one's righteousness, one's personal participation in the grace of God against all the assaults of evil. In Irenaeus, this language of individualistic asceticism must be replaced by another one, a language which emphasizes our incorporation in Christ and our solidarity as members of Christ.

Essentially, it is in this context that our thinking on the 'communion of saints' must be put. Our righteousness is first of all linked to our belonging to Christ – a belonging which is the work of the Spirit. How are we to understand this?

I have just used a word which we often come across nowadays, *solidarity*. The word itself does not belong to Irenaeus' vocabulary, but he uses another word – rather – an image, to convey that very idea; 'the dough.' It is directly drawn from the New Testament: "The kingdom of heaven" in Matthew 13:33 and "Get rid of the old yeast, so that you may be a new unleavened batch of dough" in 1 Cor. 5:6. How does Irenaeus use this image of the dough? First, he recalls how the Spirit came down upon the disciples at Pentecost – an event that had the power to admit them 'to the entrance of life' and fill them with a like spirit. Moreover, thanks to this same Spirit, all nations were brought together in unity, in the person of all those who welcomed them.

When Irenaeus refers to those who were baptized on the day of Pentecost as 'the first-fruits of all nations' offered by the Spirit to the Father, he suggests that these first Christians did not merely represent all the nations of the world, but that the different peoples themselves were going to and had to follow the same path. They too, were destined to become one in Christ by the Spirit. Once he has established this idea, Irenaeus carries on, "*Wherefore also the Lord promised to send the Comforter, who should join us to God. For as a compacted lump of dough cannot be formed of dry wheat without fluid matter, nor can a loaf possess unity, so, in like manner, neither could we, being many, be made one in Christ Jesus without the water from heaven.*" (A.H. Bk III, 17: 2)

Like a lump of dough, our humanity is sanctified by the yeast that is Christ. As for the 'Water' from heaven, it is undoubtedly the Spirit. Thanks to the Paraclete sent by Christ, we – the dry wheat – become 'one lump of dough and one loaf.' The unity in Christ is a gift of the Spirit that manifested itself first and foremost in the work of Resurrection. Humankind is called to enter the entirety of the mystery of the Son made human. What does Irenaeus say about the communion that must exist between the members of Christ? The uniqueness of Jesus does not prevent Irenaeus from speaking of the humanity of the Son as the universal mainstay of human solidarity, which seeks, above all, to fulfill the plan inscribed in all to become the image of God.

I insist here on the part played by the humanity of the Son in this process because of what Irenaeus himself says: "*...the Word of God who dwelt in man, and became the Son of man, that He might accustom man to receive God, and God to dwell in man, according to the good pleasure of the Father.*" (A.H. Bk III, 20: 2)

Thanks to the mediation of the Incarnate Word, God gets accustomed to living with us. God comes to meet His creatures in a way that suits their earthly condition. Their sanctification is based on the need to see, to touch, and to get used to sensory information. It is in this world that God 'receives' humans so that they might, in their turn, 'receive' God. The Word became flesh to draw them, to 'convince' them to willingly accept, and in a way suitable to them, the plan inscribed in their creation. This is a rather extraordinary view of things. Irenaeus suggests that we are entirely free to accept, or not, the habit of living in the presence of our Lord. He also implies that the communion with the divine leaves intact the autonomy of the created when it communes with God, a communion which does not absorb humanity, which does not assimilate it into the divine.

Perhaps there is another point to be made in the same context. If 'to be in the image of God' does not mean to lose one's autonomy and specificity, what does 'to be like Christ' mean? Is holiness just a matter of conforming to a model? Is the 'righteous' somebody who resembles the Lord in the correctness of his life?

I think that it can be said, without hesitation, that the likeness to the Word is other than a mere intellectual response. Holiness and righteousness require the commitment of the whole being to the person of the Son – the correctness of one's life bears witness to this commitment. Irenaeus did not fall into the trap of the conformity to a model making the imitation of Christ on earth the type of holiness expected or propounded by Christianity. Because of his doctrine of the incorruptibility, the achievement of perfection or fulfillment, lies more in a life in Christ than in a simple imitation of Christ. The human project to resemble the Son, is quite other than the passive and external duplication of a common model. This resemblance consists essentially in a process of internalization of divine knowledge and life. We shall come back to this subject when dealing with the resurrection and eternal life. For the moment, we can very briefly consider the perfect way of communing with God, which is also destined to contribute to the perfection of the ecclesial body as a communion of saints – martyrdom.

For the Christians in the early centuries, martyrdom proved that God was at work in his Church. Seeing in the very flesh of the Christian the features of the true martyr, Christ, they could no longer doubt the presence of His grace. One must be very precise about this. In Irenaeus, what is at stake is not the mere moral imitation of Christ, but a revelation, a 'theophany' of the deep meaning of Christian baptism. Martyrdom was seen as a true testimony of the church, the supreme testimony, par excellence, of the mission assigned to all Baptized to proclaim the Good News. How is that?

Let us recall what Irenaeus says about the Incarnate Word: He is the principle of life because He sends the Spirit. But, at his baptism, he himself was sent by the Spirit to bring the Good News to all. This is essential because the anointing that Jesus received at his baptism is not just a sign of his divinity given to humanity. This anointing of the Spirit, this descent of the Spirit upon Jesus, is considered by Irenaeus as the beginning of our possession by the Spirit. The meaning of our baptism as the vocation to proclaim the Good News starts with the baptism of Christ. In the same way that the Word, anointed by the Spirit, went to the end of his missionary vocation, the martyr – bearing also the mark of anointment by the Spirit – chooses to live up to the ultimate meaning of baptism in the testimony of his death.

It would be difficult to overstate the emphasis which the Early Church put on the anointing of Christ confirmed by martyrdom in the flesh of His own. By their death, the martyrs confirm the vocation they received not only to live by the Spirit, but also to testify before the others and bear witness for them what kind of life it means. When the 'seal of eternal life' received in baptism is tempered in the fire and blood of martyrdom, the disciple becomes really worthy of this anointing and of the name that it confers on him, Christian. In other words, the martyr's testimony is the ultimate way of proclaiming the Good News that humanity is created in the image and likeness of God. The communion of saints is, first and foremost, communion between all those bearing the seal, the mark of their belonging to Christ, as the sign of their vocation to be in His image.

By his baptism, the Christian receives the anointing of the Holy Spirit and is considered as the one bearing "the image and superscription of the Father and the Son". This is literally what Irenaeus says (*A.H. Bk III, 17: 3*). The Christians bear the Divine image in them so that they may truly actualize the sign of their belonging to God. Gradually, they must conform to the image of what they are. Yet the flesh is weak, as the Christians destined to endure the hardship of the arena were to know. For the flesh to be faithful to the vocation inscribed in it, *"The weakness of the flesh will be absorbed by the strength of the Spirit; and that the man in whom this takes place cannot in that case be carnal, but spiritual; because of the fellowship of the Spirit. Thus it is, therefore, that the martyrs bear their witness, and despise death, not after the infirmity of the flesh, but because of the readiness of the Spirit."* (*A.H. Bk V, 9: 2*).

A careful reading of Irenaeus' thinking here shows an unexpected but very strong link between creation and baptism, of which martyrdom, that of Christ first, then that of his disciples, is the perfect revelation of its meaning. Human beings, created to be in the image of God, are regenerated in the water of Baptism to confirm the purpose of their creation. (One understands why 'confirmation' was considered as the crowning of the baptismal ceremony and not as a separate sacrament in the early Church!) First of all, Baptism is the restoration – or the recapitulation – of creation. There is perfect coincidence between the beginning (generation) and baptism (regeneration). Every time the Church baptizes, it acknowledges the fact that matter, the clay from which the human body was made, is part of the vocation of humans to be in the image of God. This flesh, so weak at the beginning, is destined to know the strength of the Spirit in glory. And, when it is the victory of the martyr over 'the weakness of the flesh,' it is the whole Church that benefits from this victory. The church is seen as reinforced and confirmed as 'the communion of saints.' This is one of the fundamental tenets of Irenaeus' ecclesiology. It is quite knowingly that he expresses his conviction that God's righteousness (holiness) will not only manifest itself in the fulfillment of His image in each of the members of Christ, but also in the Church in its entirety. (He saw the weak, the renegades in his own Church, return to the true life of the Spirit!) *"God thus determining all things beforehand for the bringing of man to perfection, for his edification, and for the revelation of His dispensations, that goodness may both be made apparent, and righteousness perfected, and that the Church may be fashioned after the image of His Son."* *(A.H. Bk IV, 37: 7)*

Here we are dealing with something essential: the fullness of life in the Spirit for the baptized is not given once and for all, but it is to be arrived at after a long dynamic process. The Church conforms to its Head in so far as its members live up to the gift of charity in their lives. Now for Irenaeus, this charity is made manifest in martyrdom because of its meaning for the community. Let us recall that Irenaeus seeks to refute heresies that threaten to tear apart the unity and communion of the Church. In his eyes, heresy is a true crime against God's love because, in his stubbornness, the heretic is ready to 'tear apart and divide the body of Christ' in order to maintain his own doctrine. One understands better why Irenaeus holds martyrs in such high esteem, when one thinks of those whose doctrines destroyed so much. The martyr is more than the mere outward manifestation of a vigorous spiritual life in an individual. The death of a martyr is the most blatant sign of holiness and charity in the Church: *"The Church does in every place, because of that love which she cherishes towards God, send forward, throughout all time, a multitude of martyrs to the Father." (A.H. Bk IV, 33: 9)*. The Church, which is constantly mutilated by the 'false Gnosis,' lives anew through its martyrs. It grows by its members and recovers its integrity thanks to martyrs who, by defending the true Gnosis of the apostles to the death, overthrow the process of destruction loosed by heresy. Their death is the perfect example of a healthy, efficient, and vivifying predication.

What Irenaeus says about the meaning of martyrdom can perfectly be applied to the way the bishop must bear witness in the Church for which he is responsible.

The Meaning of "Exemplary Conduct" of the Bishop

The deep affinity between the Church and its mission of proclaiming the Good News by the witness of its own members has quite practical consequences in Irenaeus' thinking. People do not need to seek in vain before knowing the truth, the truth proclaimed in the Good News. This truth is given by the Spirit in the Church with the proclamation of the word of the Scriptures.

This is why Irenaeus sees in preaching, as much as in martyrdom, an essential witness of the faith and an indispensable component of its growth. The apostles, the prophets, and the doctors were given to the Church by the Spirit inspiring them so that the truth may be preached and made known. But, we must be aware that 'to preach' goes far beyond a Sunday sermon! Irenaeus clearly says that the task of the presbyters of the Church is to preserve and teach entirely 'neither receiving addition nor curtailment' to what it has received from the apostles. *"The Word (of God) must be read without falsification, and (with) a lawful and diligent exposition in harmony with the Scriptures, both without danger and without blasphemy."* *(A.H. Bk IV, 33: 8)*

This responsibility of the bishops has nothing to do with a 'power' or 'magisterial authority.' The true reading of the Scriptures is a charism – it is linked to the greatest of all charisms, namely charity. To ensure the faithful transmission of faith is an act of charity. Now there again, Irenaeus sees this responsibility in a non-legal context. One does not automatically achieve a 'true reading' of the Scriptures just because one is a bishop. Irenaeus links the integrity of the Word to the integrity of the life of the preacher. He tells the Christians to learn the truth *"...from those who possess that succession of the Church which is from the apostles, (the presbyters) and among whom exists that which is sound and blameless in conduct, as well as that which is unadulterated and incorrupt in speech."* *(A.H. Bk IV, 26: 5)*. Here are the three criteria of an authentic Episcopal function:

1. The succession of bishops from the apostles
2. Integrity in conduct
3. Faithfulness to the preached Word.

There is nothing surprising in the bringing together of these three criteria if one remembers that, for Irenaeus, the knowledge of God must be shown in the acknowledgment of the Son, that is to say, in the likeness to Him. More than anyone else, in his own life the bishop must show the truth of the Word which he is expected to transmit. There is more than a mere moral exhortation here. It is truly a necessity, a vital need for the Church. The truth with which it has been trusted must not be kept hidden and invisible. It would have no effect on people who, because of their human condition, *need to see achieved what they have been told.* The Church is a visible body. It testifies openly, before everyone, the reality of the presence of its

Head when it guarantees the truth that it proclaims by a conduct that is beyond reproach.

In this, we have another example of righteousness as being a service, an example of holiness at the service of communion: in the same way that the Word of God manifested itself before humanity in order to be seen and understood, likewise the believers, particularly the bishops, must show by their own lives the truth of God's life, which is the source of all holiness in themselves. It seems to me that this way of considering the Episcopal function in the Church is extremely important to rid the succession of the bishops of any legal interpretation. Nothing is done automatically; the Episcopal function is a charisma. The integrity of the bishop's conduct and the purity of his word are ministries of charity, because their function is to draw the attention of the Baptized towards the One who is the source of their lives. In no way is the bishop to be considered as a dignitary, a figure to whom honor is due. Far from drawing the attention to his own person, his exemplary conduct is, in some way, symbolic since it directs the faithful to their true source of unity and communion, Christ. That is why it is perfectly legitimate, I think, to speak of the Episcopal function as one of the essential components of the 'communion of saints.'

The Holiness of the Church and the Spirit

Let us pay attention to this complete phrase of Irenaeus', which is often quoted and commented upon: *"For where the Church is, there is the Spirit of God; and where the Spirit of God is, there is the Church, and every kind of grace." (A.H. Bk III, 24: 1)*

We have just seen the Episcopal function as something dynamic from the very fact that it directs us to Christ at work within us. The same dynamic prevails here. A static view of the Church would be very difficult to bring into line with this way of speaking of the relationship between the Church and the Spirit. In order to understand Irenaeus, one must do away with the image of the Church, with its curia, its baptismal registers, and all its institutional machinery. With Irenaeus, we are in another world. For him, *the Church is none other than the Spirit of Christ at work everywhere in the world and in the hearts of everyone*. It is the Spirit that delineates the true limits of the Church. Implicit here in this vision of things is the idea that the true members of Christ are essentially those who live by His spirit. This is why it is up to the Spirit to take a 'census' of them, as Irenaeus says. The true members of Christ are listed by the Spirit!

This way of viewing the Church is in no way contradictory to the idea that the Baptized gather together to live as a community. Much to the contrary. Let us recall the Irenaean principle that humans, because of their carnal condition, need to see, to hear, and to touch. A purely spiritual Church, disembodied, would be unthinkable for Irenaeus. If it is impossible to fix the limits of ecclesia because of the Spirit that makes the church present everywhere, this does not avoid her need to visibly bear witness to the mediation of the Spirit in a community. The Spirit opens the Church as an entrance to life, that is to say, as something visible. It is what Irenaeus says, *"For she is the entrance to life."* (A.H. Bk III,4: 1) The Church is not life, but it is the way to life since the Lord entrusted her with the 'rule of truth,' the faith of the apostles.

On several occasions, Irenaeus uses the phrase 'the synagogues of God' (*for instance, A.H. Bk III, 6: 1*) to refer to the groups of baptized who, thanks to the Spirit's anointment, become true communities of the adopted sons of the Father. The expression 'the synagogues of God' is interesting because it calls to mind the custom of the Early Church to refer to itself thus in order to highlight its awareness of being the fulfillment of Jewish hope. 'The synagogue of God' was a quote from the book of Deuteronomy, 'the synagogue of Yahweh.' The Christian community considered themselves to be the continuation and achievement of that of Sinai. In short, what does all this mean?

I see four points to highlight:

• The Church is indeed a people, the people of God gathering before Him.

• It is therefore visible; it leads its life in the open (nothing is secret).

• The Church does not exist for itself; it directs all its members to the One who makes them children whose adoption consists of communion with one another and with God.

• The Church is essentially open, whereas a people who close their borders and close in on themselves, run the risk – often borne out by history – of suffocation.

In the end, *the fundamental tension between synagogue and diaspora is to be acknowledged and accepted as an essential feature of the communion of saints.*

This is true of the Jewish people. It is also true of the new synagogues of God which make up the Church. Where the Church is, there is the Spirit of God, and where the Spirit of God is, there is the Church in all grace. It is thus impossible, from this viewpoint, to speak about membership criteria or limits to the work of the Spirit moving each of us to be in communion with the adopted children of the Father. And if this communion is not fully achieved before death, it will be the case in the kingdom of the Son, as we have seen. This is, I think, the reason for Irenaeus' emphasis on the 'earnest of the Spirit,' which we receive in our life on earth. The communion of saints is not a static reality, a perfect datum, or a work accomplished once and for all. It is a people, sometimes gathered together, sometimes in the diaspora, which has received the 'earnest of the Spirit,' that is to say the necessary participation in the life of God that inclines and prepares this people in advance to live the glory of God. What comes out of Irenaeus' vision here is quite coherent with his principle that all beginnings are frail. The anointing by the Spirit is but a beginning. It makes humans progress in God's ways especially when baptism is experienced and confirmed in a 'synagogue of God,' in a local Church, where the effects of baptism are reinforced by the Eucharist.

When the seed of life, which the Word is, takes root in humans, it makes them partake in the flesh of Christ and thus secures the filial adoption making it grow more and more in the Baptized (and in no way is 'adoption' static or legal: one becomes more and more the child one is!). This dynamic relationship between the Eucharist and the anointing by the Spirit is clearly stated by Irenaeus himself: *"The Bread of immortality, which is the Spirit of the Father."* (A.H. IV, 38: 1). Now, the context of this statement brings to mind the child in need of food in order to grow. The Eucharist is the means chosen by the Lord to give Himself to humans who are still too weak to bear the greatness of His glory. The communion with the flesh of the Lord gradually makes human flesh participate in the incorruptibility of the children of God. This is why Irenaeus calls the Eucharist 'the bread of immortality.' And, if he also calls it 'Spirit of the Father,' this is because he sees there 'the earnest of the Spirit' preparing the people of God to bear His glory. ■

CHAPTER IX

I Believe in the Forgiveness of Sins

Why has God allowed humans to sin? Why does he let some commit evil deeds and harm others? Is there a more mysterious side to our existence on earth than sin and evil? Jesus himself did not give us an explanation for evil. He suffered its consequences and triumphed over it, not by eliminating human potential for sin but by destroying its absolute nature. We are not inevitably and forever condemned to live in sin – and this because forgiveness and reconciliation do exist. This is the final teaching that Jesus left with us as he died.

This is wonderful. This would help us greatly to put things in perspective if we could really believe in the truthfulness of this teaching and live up to it. But, life is not all that simple and we go on suffering evil as a scandal – and committing evil as something almost inevitable and irresistible. We clearly understand Saint Paul when he says, "I do not understand what I do. For what I want to do I do not do, but what I hate I do… it is no longer I myself who does it, but it is sin living in me." (Romans 7:15-17)

Basically, could it be that the sinful condition that we feel so intensely arises from our conviction that we are made for something greater than ourselves? We acknowledge that there is something in us that is out of tune with God. We really do not know why, but we feel the contradiction deeply in our being. While we are out of tune with God, we know that we are made for Him. It seems to me that in saying this, I am not too far removed from Irenaeus' thinking.

When dealing with the mystery of evil, Irenaeus seems, like us, to be at a loss to provide an explanation as we have already seen in chapter VI. As for sin, Adam's sin, he feels more at ease, if I may say so. This is also true for our own personal sins.

When one looks closely at everything Irenaeus says about the sinner, it is clear that, like us, he believes in the 'forgiveness of sins' even though nowhere does he mention what we call the 'sacrament of forgiveness' or even the 'power to forgive sins.' All this sacramental theology belongs to a later period.

For instance, the confession of sins mentioned in the Didache is not a 'sacramental confession' but a sort of communal prayer uttered by all the participants in the assemblies of the community. When some had sinned deeply (murder, adultery, apostasy...) they were excluded from the Eucharist, they were subject to fraternal correction on the part of the community, and they were thought to be reconciled with God after having proven themselves by works of penance: conversion, prayer, tears, fasting, giving alms.

How does Irenaeus view Adam, the first sinner? It is principally through his teaching about Adam that we best understand what human sin was for Irenaeus and how the sinner was to behave in the eyes of God in order to be forgiven.

THE UNFINISHED NATURE OF HUMANS AT ODDS WITH THEIR FULFILLMENT

"His hands formed a living man, in order that Adam might be created (again) after the image and likeness of God." (A.H. Bk V, 1: 3)

The meaning of this text is perfectly clear; the two Hands of God, the Word and the Spirit, have inscribed in humanity a future, or better, a plan for growth. But, not just any plan! Humans are called to complete the image and likeness of God after whom they were created. But, to speak of completeness is to speak of distance, of space, and an interval between a beginning and an end – in a word, *history*. Thanks to the spatio-temporal dimension inscribed in God's creation, Adam and his descendants gradually become 'fully alive.'

Of course, Irenaeus says that, *"…it was possible for God Himself to have made man perfect from the first, but man could not receive this (perfection), being as yet an infant." (A.H. Bk IV, 38:1).*

For this reason, God *"…formed him for growth and increase"* *(A.H. Bk IV, 11:1).*

Man must thus grow in perfection. This is the reason for his freedom as follows: *"…man is possessed of free will from the beginning." (A.H. Bk IV, 37:4)*

However, let us not be mistaken; the freedom he uses to reach perfection has its limits. This is why there are limits to the harm humans can do to themselves by a misuse of their freedom. In order to understand this way of thinking about freedom in Irenaeus, it is clear that the image of Adam as a child plays a major role. It shows that freedom is nothing abstract but it manifests itself in a being of flesh, in a being who has not yet reached maturity and, consequently, lacks good judgment. It means that the ill-use of freedom is deplorable – even tragic – but not really 'abnormal.' We are not surprised to hear Irenaeus speak of Adam's sin in terms which bring to mind the 'growing pains' of an adolescent.

This is what Henri Rondet thinks: "Man according to Irenaeus is…an adolescent geared towards the future and whose ills, whose very mistakes are only growing pains." Consequently, "his rebellion against God's orders, reprehensible rebellion of course, looks more like the whims of a child, rather than the pride of a demon."[25] Irenaeus says, "*Man…inadvertently and not out of wickedness* [26] *became involved in disobedience. As for God, He took compassion upon man.*" (*A.H. Bk IV, 40: 3*).

God's compassion towards Adam is best understood if we take into account the lack of experience and ignorance of the latter. Indeed, Adam enjoyed far less 'leeway' than Satan in temptation. In addition, he responded to the gift of forgiveness granted to him by God. Beguiled by the pretext of immortality, *"He is immediately seized with terror, and hides himself, not as if he were able to escape from God; but, in a state of confusion at having transgressed His command, he feels unworthy to appear before and to hold converse with God."* (*A.H. Bk III, 23: 5*)

The important point here is Irenaeus' insistence on the salvation of Adam: *"But inasmuch as man is saved, it is fitting that he who was created the original man should be saved. For it is too absurd to maintain, that he who was so deeply injured by the enemy, and was the first to suffer captivity, was not rescued by Him who conquered the enemy."* (*A.H. Bk III, 23: 2*)

---

25   Henri Rondet, *Le Péché originel dans la tradition patristique et théologique*, Paris Fayard, 1966, p. 49-50.

26   The English translation by Alexander Roberts and William Rambaut has been slightly modified in order to match the French translation from the Greek. See Translators' note at the end of the book, page 200.

It is particularly the way he thinks of Christ's work of recapitulation that allows Irenaeus to assert so forcefully Adam's salvation: *"It was necessary, therefore, that the Lord, coming to the lost sheep, and making recapitulation of so comprehensive a dispensation, and seeking after His own handiwork, should save that very man who had been created after His image and likeness, that is, Adam." (A.H. Bk III, 23: 1); "For never at any time did Adam escape the hands of God." (A.H. Bk V, 1: 3); "He pronounced no curse against Adam personally." (A.H. Bk III, 23: 3).*

These are the reasons, among others, that enable us to say with confidence that Irenaeus does not view Adam's sin as a catastrophic event either for himself or for his descendants. With Irenaeus, his sin is quite different from 'the original sin' that Augustine will insist on later! Because Irenaeus is not indifferent to the unfathomable mystery of the heart locked in sin, he does not borrow the idea that Adam's sin would be the cause for the permanent presence of sin in humans, or more precisely the hard and unrepentant sin within themselves. On the contrary, Irenaeus' analysis of Adam's sin implies elements of great hope that we could highlight better with a brief critical review.

Humans Always Have 'Free Access' to God

The figure of Adam, as seen by Irenaeus, provides food for thought as it is particularly revealing of the ambiguity of the human condition and of sin in general. The criterion that drives us to assess the relevance for faith of what comes from the outside perfectly conforms to Irenaeus' teaching about the sin of Adam. For the bishop of Lyon, the sin of the first human is always shown as a prideful act, as his refusal to admit his limited nature. If Adam is created in the image of God, he must consider this honor as a gift, as a plan, and not a right.

Challenging the Gnostics who believed themselves to be naturally spiritual, perfect, and immortal, Irenaeus points to the very root of sin, not only of Adam but of us all. A human being should not be deceived, that is to say, should not behave like a Gnostic for whom incorruptible life is a right. A human should not consider "...*that the incorruptibility which belongs to him is his own naturally, and by thus not holding the truth, should boast with empty superciliousness, as if he were naturally like to God. For he (Satan) thus rendered him (man) more ungrateful towards his Creator, obscured the love which God had towards man, and blinded his mind not to perceive what is worthy of God, comparing himself with, and judging himself equal to God."* (A.H. Bk III, 20: 1)

What is striking in this text is the pernicious character of sin. It blinds humans as to their nature made for God and leads them to the fiction of believing the lie according to which they are not accountable to anybody. Being created for life, they believe they can take charge of this plan themselves and ensure its fulfillment by their own efforts. It is as if they believed God less able than themselves to bring about its fulfillment. Thus understood, the pride of the sinner is essentially an absurd stance. Worse, it points to a significant lack of coherence because sin denies the true nature of humanity.

It is in this context that Irenaeus helps us understand the meaning of the tree in the Adamic story. Sign of the forbidden, the tree marks the necessary limits for humans not to be deceived as to the truth of their finite nature. It is not about refusing humans all access to God, but about making them progress gradually towards God, in their own way. On this issue, Irenaeus clearly explains his viewpoint. Humans must have access to God, but not just in any way. They must abide by the limits of nature as created;

"But, lest man should conceive thoughts too high, and be exalted and uplifted, as though he had no lord, because of the authority and freedom granted to him, and so should transgress against his maker God, over-passing his measure, and entertain selfish imaginings of pride in opposition to God; a law was given to him by God... He set him certain limitations, so that, if he should keep the commandment of God, he should ever remain such as he was, that is to say, immortal; but, if he should not keep it, he should become mortal." (Dem.15)

In this text, Irenaeus focuses essentially on two ideas: On the one hand, God is always accessible to humans, and on the other hand, He imposes limits on them. At first glance, this standpoint is incomprehensible. It seems self-contradictory to support humans' yearning for happiness while imposing limits on them. This would be perfectly right if one opposed the 'prideful thought,' which works on the level of inner consciousness, to God's commandment seen as something exterior to humans, that is to say as a sort of arbitrary 'natural law.' It would be comparable to the idea sometimes put forward, according to which God, out of jealousy, would have forbidden the tree to Adam. He would have barred human beings from the path to happiness so that they would not know the secrets of the gods. Indeed, in such a case the transgression should be looked upon as a sin of *hubris* in the Greek sense, that is to say, the movement of the human soul which, out of immoderation, outrages the gods, disrupts the intangible order of the cosmos, and thus becomes God's rival.

Irenaeus certainly does not share this opinion as he explicitly says that humans have free access to God. His viewpoint can be understood provided that the human desire, always to go further, is considered as compatible with binding limits. In other words, the difficulty disappears if these limits are simply equated with humans' finite nature. If one accepts this way of seeing things, the interdiction turns into a condition for opportunity. It rekindles the thirst for the infinite which is no longer based on pride or the unrestrained confidence in oneself, but rather on the Other, that is to say, on God Himself.

This is the true 'access' to God. By renouncing fulfillment through their own efforts only, humans accept fulfillment through the One who is the very foundation of their being. With confidence and humility, they accept the plan inscribed in their creation to become fully what they are, not by achieving this against God or in spite of Him, but through Him. Thus, their limited nature becomes the medium for their transformation. The frontier between God and humanity reveals itself to be an opening. It can be said that for Irenaeus, human longing is firmly grounded if we view it according to his teaching about humans as being 'the form of God' in their very flesh.

The sign and guarantee of God's accessibility, the image of God in humans, is fully consistent with its vocation of being for human beings their 'principle of growth.' This means that, contrary to 'the impatient' who do not accept their unfinished nature, the 'form of God' in a being made of flesh puts sin within the global movement of its growth. The impatient, says Irenaeus, "*...wish to be even now like God their Creator (...they... insist) that there is no distinction between the uncreated God and man, a creature of today.*" (A.H. Bk IV, 38: 4)

Here we have one of the important facets of the experience of sin, to allow God's mercy to work within the sinner in a pedagogical way, that is to say, as the knowledge that puts humans back on their feet. In this, God's merciful love acts as an antidote to the bitterness that overwhelms sinners as they find themselves fallible and capable even of the worst. What is expected from humans is not perfection, but hearts open to the work of improvement achieved in them through the salutary experience of sin and forgiveness. "This, therefore, was the (object of the) long-suffering of God, that man, passing through all things, and acquiring…and (learning) by experience what is the source of his deliverance, while…he may think of God in accordance with the divine greatness."

Irenaeus concludes, *"For he who holds, without pride and boasting, the true glory regarding created things and the Creator… continuing in His love and subjection, and giving of thanks, shall also receive from Him the greater glory of promotion, looking forward to the time when he shall become like Him who died for him." (A.H. Bk III, 20: 2)*

Thus, God expects from all humans, as from Adam, that they acknowledge the true source of their perfection and happiness. Let them know that the integrity of their being as an image of God remains intact and this because God does not accept that the work of his Hands be destroyed. The power of His love, stronger than the sin of humans, does not allow them to fall into the claws of evil forever. Such is the lesson of hope pervading Irenaeus' reading of the Adamic story. ■

CHAPTER X

I Believe in the Resurrection of the Flesh and Life Everlasting

The Resurrection of the Flesh

"That the paternal light might meet with and rest upon the flesh of our Lord, and come to us from His resplendent flesh, and that thus man might attain to immortality, having been invested with the paternal light." (A.H. Bk IV, 20: 2)

In this short text, we have the gist of Irenaeus' teaching on this article of the Apostles' Creed. Human beings in their entirety and not only their souls attain incorruptibility. They are not incorruptible by nature. It is thanks to the Incarnation, thanks to the flesh of the Son resplendent with the light of the Father, that humans attain incorruptibility.

These are basic assertions as regards the resurrection of the flesh. Let us try to understand them in the light of Irenaeus' thinking.

Humans are Not Incorruptible by Nature

Irenaeus speaks at length of the incorruptibility of the flesh, of its resurrection, and of its everlasting life after death. The historical reason for this is not hard to understand. It was to refute the Gnostic idea according to which the spiritual being was incorruptible and divine by nature. In other words, for the Gnostics, incorruptibility is not a gift of God but something quite normal because of the relationship between the spiritual and God. Still one must specify here, it is as spiritual beings – as souls – that the Gnostics consider themselves to be incorruptible. Their fleshly bodies are but containers that they discard while returning to the celestial spheres, to the Perfect Father. The return to the Father starts with the leaving behind of the body since matter is not susceptible to be saved.

How does one challenge this viewpoint which is obviously at odds with the Christian faith? Not only does the Gnostic standpoint deny human wholeness and hence the participation of the flesh in the glory of God, but also the necessity of Incarnation as warranty of the future incorruptibility of the risen. Irenaeus keeps harking back to this issue in order to clarify the teaching handed down from the apostles.

First of all, like us, he acknowledges that humans are not incorruptible by nature. Without the Creator's deliberate intervention, their bodies would return to the 'dust' from which they were created. But truly, such an intervention is not at all clear to us due to our experience of death! Neither was it for Irenaeus. He saw too well the consequences of death. Because of our mortal nature, we are subject to the natural forces of dissolution, forces which dislocate the forces of growth. Thus, incorruptibility cannot result from a quasi-biological process. It must be understood in a different way, without denying what faith teaches us; resurrection is about humans in their entirety and not only their spirituality. Incorruptibility must be considered as a component of the historical nature of humanity, without being natural or due to this nature. This is a fundamental assertion in Irenaeus because no human being is complete where there is only a discarnate body. [27] Incorruptibility truly involves humans in their fleshly bodies. Moreover, it must not be considered as an addition, something abnormal or alien to humanity

What then can be said about incorruptibility? If it is a component of the historical nature of humanity without being naturally produced by this nature, how are we supposed to understand it?

As one might have expected, and because of the ruling principle of all his thinking, Irenaeus views it in terms of growth. In fact, he views incorruptibility as a gift, an intervention that happened at the very moment of creation. Right at the beginning of their creation in the image and likeness of God and because of their being an image of God (and in keeping with this nature), humans received the gift of incorruptibility, or more precisely, the 'earnest' of incorruptible life. This is what they are directed towards. Incorruptibility, in its fullness, is only to be given at the end. It is a gift that starts with the beginnings of humanity but which then reveals itself as a tangible and confirmed gift only at the end when humans are mature enough to see and apprehend God. 'Created in the image of God' implies for Irenaeus, a long maturation for human beings, thanks to which they fully achieve their project to be in the likeness of the Son. Finally, humans enter incorruptibility because they become the image of

---

27 Irenaeus sets out to expose the Gnostics' arguments about the survival of the soul by telling them that this would be a kind of incomplete existence and that anyway, in spite of the dissolution of the body, the soul would continue to preserve the very character of the body. This is why the idea of reincarnation must be rejected, he says. (See A.H. Bk II, 33 to 34:1)

the Son and because communion with the Son naturally ends in the same condition of incorruptibility as that of The Risen Lord.

This last assertion is particularly important. The participation of humanity in the resplendence of the glorified flesh of Christ does not alter human nature, but achieves the fulfillment of a process that began here below at the very beginnings of humanity. Incorruptibility is the accomplishment of what started in history, of what was in the beginning a frail sketch of what awaits humans.

With Irenaeus, of course, this view of things rests on the idea that life is one single reality. In his thinking, there is not a 'natural life' without God, and then a second 'spiritual life' or 'supernatural life' that would be reserved for humans living in 'a state of grace' and which would somehow be an addition to their natural lives. For Irenaeus, there is but one life, frail of course in its beginnings, but destined to be gradually 'stabilized,' so to speak, with a greater and greater participation in the life of the Lord. This is a dynamic view of the God-Human relationship. Incorruptibility is the natural outcome of our life, our life begun here below and made firmer and firmer because of its gradual progress towards divine life.

This is a wonderful teaching which brings solace, but it removes nothing of the reality of death. How are we to understand this lesson about the incorruptibility of humans in relation to the coming and reality of death? How can one speak of the incorruptibility of the flesh which is obviously destined to dissolution? What light does Irenaeus throw on this issue? This is to be found, I think, in his theology of the Spirit, the warranty of life.

The Growth of Life Until Incorruptibility
Let us begin with a key passage on this issue:

"By this arrangement, therefore, and these harmonies, and a sequence of this nature, man, a created and organized being, is rendered after the image and likeness of the uncreated God – the Father planning everything well and giving His commands, the Son carrying these into execution and performing the work of creating, and the Spirit nourishing and increasing [what is made], but man making progress day by day, and ascending towards the perfect, that is, approximating to the uncreated One. For the Uncreated is perfect, that is, God. Now it was necessary that man should in the first instance be created; and having been created, should receive growth; and having received growth, should be strengthened; and having been strengthened, should abound; and having abounded, should recover (from the disease of sin); and having recovered, should be glorified; and being glorified, should see his Lord. For God is He who is yet to be seen, and the beholding of God is productive of immortality, but immortality renders one near unto God." (A.H. Bk IV, 38: 3)

In this passage, where there are many noteworthy points, I choose to highlight the following: thanks to the Spirit, source of nourishment and growth, human beings make progress step-by-step and ascend to perfection, which makes them and their lives incorruptible. All of human life, from infancy to its passage to incorruptible life through death, is directed to this end. What gives coherence to this way of thinking, is on the one hand, the fact that for Irenaeus life is one (humans live on the biological, ethical, psychic, spiritual levels, etc.; there are not several kinds of 'lives') and on the other hand, this life is nothing other than the creation of human beings in the image of God. Because they are made in the image of God and because it is unthinkable that this image might one day disappear, humanity will live forever. It remains to be seen how. Human beings cannot remain in the vulnerability of infancy. Here, the role of the Spirit is to nourish them and make them grow so that the image of

God, which they are, might appear more and more clearly. In the end, the glory of the image of God in humans transfigures them in their very flesh, hence their incorruptible nature.

Of course, such a viewpoint would be totally incomprehensible if life were to be taken as a mere empirical datum, totally identified with the vital forces of the body. Irenaeus' vision is essentially biblical: the life breathed into Adam's nostrils and the uncreated life of the Spirit are not two separate lives, but divine life in which humans gradually take part. Right from the beginning, the Spirit takes hold of them in order to work on them, to prepare them for the incorruptibility which will transform their entire being (*See A.H. Bk V, 12: 4*), and this is true for all human beings. Indeed, some do nothing to participate actively in the growth of the Spirit within them, even quite the contrary sometimes. The life by which they live, is little or badly developed – a bit like a gift or a talent which is ill-used or not used at all. What is different for those who accept God's plan for themselves is that the power of the Spirit in them is actualized. They become active partners in a relationship set up by the Spirit when they were created.

In this respect, Irenaeus calls upon a biblical image to make his point, an image that we have already mentioned, that of the 'graft of life.' He makes a distinction between those who live according to the Spirit and those who refuse to get involved in this plan. Irenaeus compares those who, by the refusal of the Spirit, prefer to remain as 'a wild olive tree' with those who, thanks to their welcome, become 'a good olive tree.' The latter are grafted to the Spirit. The righteous have a 'fruitful' life capable of bearing many fruits going as far as the incorruptible fruit, which does not rot. As for those who remain wild olive trees, they *"become careless, and bring forth for fruit the lusts of the flesh like woody produce, (and) are rendered by their own fault, unfruitful in righteousness." (A.H. Bk V, 10: 1)*

Taken to the extreme, this image of the wild and the good olive tree can give us the impression once more that there are two sorts of life – *natural life* and *supernatural life*. But, Irenaeus is very clear on the point that the engrafting of the Spirit clears away neither the substance of our body nor the image, given to all of us at the moment of our creation, but it rids us of our former vain and sinful life. (*See A.H. Bk V, 11: 2*).

The life of the Spirit encompasses all humanity as a single entity, so to speak, in which to be a sinner, spiritual, alive, or dead depends on how just each human being is. The principle of all human life is the Spirit. If humans carry out 'the works of corruption,' the Spirit can only blow feebly through them; this is why such humans will not be able to bear incorruptible life in glory. On the contrary, if they carry out the works of the Spirit, all their limbs will be vivified, and they will truly become fully alive. This is, therefore, the dynamic of the Spirit that gradually makes humans grow fully so that they might, in the end, enjoy the very incorruptibility of God Himself.

Of course, this way of speaking about the resurrection of the flesh, as the Creed says, is a bit disconcerting, as it does not focus on resurrection as a specific event, but as something that involves the whole of human life. It is less about the moment of the resurrection of a body that has rested for many years in a grave, than about life that gradually becomes incorruptible thanks to the Spirit. Death is but a passage, a necessary passage, indeed, so that all obstacles to life may be definitively overcome, but the crux of the matter lies elsewhere. It is in this life, nourished and enriched by the Spirit until incorruptibility, until our mortal condition is fully absorbed in immortality:

"But we do now receive a certain portion of His Spirit, tending towards perfection, and preparing us for incorruption, being little by little accustomed to receive and bear God; which also the apostle terms an earnest, that is, a part of the honour which has been promised us by God... This earnest, therefore, thus dwelling in us, renders us spiritual even now, and the mortal is swallowed up by immortality... what shall it be when, on rising again, we behold Him face-to-face; when all the members shall burst out into a continuous hymn of triumph, glorifying Him who raised them from the dead, and gave the gift of eternal life? For if the earnest, gathering man into itself, does even now cause him to cry, Abba, Father, what shall the complete grace of the Spirit effect, which shall be given to men by God? It will render us like Him, and accomplish the will of the Father; for it shall make man after the image and likeness of God." (A.H. Bk V, 8: 1)

This is how Irenaeus deals with the resurrection, our faith in 'the resurrection of the flesh.' But, in this last passage, he also hints at what the life of the risen ones will be, which brings us to the last assertion of the *Creed*, everlasting life.

Everlasting Life

Let us tackle this last issue by dividing it into two parts, since everlasting life does not only refer to the saved, but also to the damned, and let us start with the latter. What does Irenaeus say about the wretched who refuse to live in the Spirit and who refuse to become what all their creation has prepared them to be, that is to say, in the image of God?

Are There any 'Damned'?

Undoubtedly, for Irenaeus, the separation between God and humans is due to the initiative of the latter. *"But on as many as, ac-*

cording to their [men] own choice, depart from God, He (God) inflicts that separation from Himself which they (men) have chosen of their own accord. But separation from God is death." (A.H. Bk V, 27: 2)

The important phrase here is surely 'their own choice.' It concerns directly one of the most formidable aspects of salvation, that is to say, the permanent tension between the universal dimension of salvation and human freedom. Because God's goodness precisely implies human autonomy faced with a vocation to become the image of God, this plan implies freedom as well. The vocation of humanity is inscribed in each of its members without exception, but it is enforced neither by an external obligation nor by an internal resolve. Yet this is not enough to solve the awesome dilemma of the apparent failure of God with respect to sinners. Irenaeus asks, *"And why is his goodness, which does not save all (thus), defective?"* (A.H. Bk IV, 33: 2)

One can well see that the plight of the wicked is something that distresses him. He cannot turn a blind eye to it. God's love and mercy do not prevent some from turning their backs on Him. Salvation does not end with Christ's personal victory since humans are free to take part in it or not. Freedom involves everyone, Christ and his members in the same battle. This is how the members of Christ gradually conform to the perfect Image of the Father, this Lord, who was the first to overcome evil. *If human mortality is overcome by immortality, as Irenaeus says, and the corruptible by the incorruptible, it is because humanity has reached the perfection of its creation as an image of God.*

Unfortunately, sin hampers the momentum of life towards incorruptibility. This assertion would not mean much, were we to forget that for Irenaeus, there is no dissociation between human life and what we call 'moral life.' At any rate, it is hardly necessary to insist upon the moral degradation that often follows sin as a consequence.

But, there is also the physical or biological decline called death. Irenaeus shows it to be also part of the consequences of sin, not as a punishment but as an inescapable consequence of our nature, which is not yet incorruptible enough to resist the damage brought about by evil. Everybody, even saints, even Christ, go through this because we are all touched by the consequences of evil. However, the ungodly, the unrepentant, and the stubborn who stick proudly with their free decision to stand apart from God – what is to become of them?

First of all, in no way does Irenaeus think of the annihilation of the reprobates as he insists on the universality of the corporeal resurrection. Everyone will rise from the dead, the wicked too. Irenaeus refers to the image of everlasting fire recalling that God prepared it for the devil and those who joined him in his apostasy (*See A.H. Bk II, 7: 3*). In this, Irenaeus echoes the Scriptures without specifying the meaning of this image by any comment on his part. In this, I think he shows wisdom. He makes no claim to know the fate of the impenitent. The biblical texts that he quotes do not mention it. Neither does Irenaeus. What is certain is that, whatever their plight, the reprobates exclude themselves from divine communion. To sum up, it is sheer madness to deny God, right to the end, since withdrawal from the light that makes one live entails absolute withdrawal from God.

"The glory of God is a Living Man; and the Life of Man Consists in Beholding God."

Now, how does Irenaeus speak of eternal life? First of all, let us recall a key idea of Irenaeus' eschatology that the beginning and the end of all things are to be found joined at their core, the Incarnate Word.

Eschatology would be the end already achieved in the Incarnate Word. All life here below in the kingdom of the Son, in glory, is recapitulated and restored in the One who is its principle and guarantor of its continuity. Christ's victory over death bears witness that nothing is lost. The Risen Son commends all, so to speak, into his Father's hands, including the world. Our material world will not disappear, but only the imperfect state that we know it to be today. Irenaeus is convinced of this.

Yet how does Irenaeus speak more precisely of everlasting life? Gradually, humanity is filled with the Spirit of Christ. Now, because the divine cannot unite with humans without making them perfect, the flesh receives the perfection of life in accordance with their being in the image of God: "*...the flesh possessed by the Spirit, forgetful indeed of what belongs to it, and adopting the quality of the Spirit, being made conformable to the Word of God.*" (A.H. Bk V, 9: 3)

From this, we see that eternal life is a specific application of the principle of growth. Irenaeus has pondered over the meaning of death and its relation to life afterwards: "*The various parts of the man, surely, which rot in the earth...these are inherited by the Spirit when they are translated into the kingdom of heaven.*" (A.H. Bk V, 9: 4)

In other words, incorruptibility does not seem to be thought of in terms of discontinuity between a corporeal body and a spiritual body, but rather as *a transition between two ways of living the same reality.* As we have seen before, life is presented as the logical outcome of the 'earnest' of the Spirit already given in earthly flesh, weak of course, but actually capable of receiving this wonderful crowning of its creation in the image of God. "*When the Spirit absorbs the weakness (of the flesh), it possesses the flesh as an inheritance in itself, and from both of these is formed a living man – living, indeed, because*

he partakes of the Spirit, but man, because of the substance of flesh."
(A.H. Bk V, 9: 2)

Given the part played by the Spirit in the transformation of humans so that they may be fully alive, one understands better the famous words of Irenaeus, often quoted but usually without the second part: *"For the glory of God is a living man; and the life of man consists in beholding God." (A.H. Bk IV, 20: 7)*

The human is always engaged in the life of God – the same human lives the same life with more and more assurance. Humans, who in their flesh, endure the suffering and conflict of terrestrial life are the very ones who will enjoy incorruptible life after death.

As for eternal life, while being a 'crowning,' it can also be more than that. For Irenaeus, death is less a severance than a *passage*. I am deliberately using the word *passage* here, because it seems to me, that it best illustrates his deep intuition that death is anything but the end of a process of growth. It is not the dividing line beyond which the progress toward God would be impossible. Rather, death is the opening of a new area for the exercise of freedom, now confirmed in its inclination towards God. Death marks the end of sin, the true obstacle to human progress and the cause of misery. With death, human growth is no longer hindered: *"For we do never cease from loving God; but in proportion as we continue to contemplate Him, so much the more do we love Him." (A.H. Bk IV, 12: 2)*

It is an extraordinary idea because it means that life after death should be a tremendous adventure. We will never stop knowing God; we shall continue approaching Him for eternity.

Here, Death would be freedom set free. This means that freedom is less the right to choose between good and evil than the capacity for humans fully to live up to their nature. From this point of view, death would not be the end of freedom but the ultimate liberation of humans, *the ultimate liberation of their freedom*. With Death, there would be nothing left to prevent the progress of life towards incorruptibility. Humans will be freed, so to speak, of everything that resists their liberation so that they may follow their liberator, Christ, the Firstborn from the dead.

Yet again, let us listen to Irenaeus who makes a very strong connection between these two ideas, that of a freedom set free to keep faith in Christ more than ever and that of a never-ending and unhindered move towards God in glory. *"For He did not set us free for this purpose, that we should depart from Him (no one, indeed, while placed out of reach of the Lord's benefits, has power to procure for himself the means of salvation), but that the more we receive His grace, the more we should love Him. Now the more we have loved Him, the more glory shall we receive from Him, when we are continually in the presence of the Father."* (A.H. Bk IV, 13: 3)

Freedom is thus necessary in order to love, to keep faith in the Lord. It is even more so after death, after the final freeing of humanity from all sin. Irenaeus gives us the impression that freedom is necessary, precisely in order to progress in the knowledge and love of God after death. *"For as God is always the same, so also man, when found in God, shall always go on towards God. For neither does God at any time cease to confer benefits upon, or to enrich man."* (A.H. Bk IV, 11: 2)

"Ready for incorruptibility, 'the new man shall remain (continually), always holding fresh converse with God.' And since (or, that) these things shall ever continue without end, Isaiah declares..." (A.H. Bk V, 36: 1)

Clearly, Irenaeus dismisses here any idea of a static perfection, achieved once and for all. To say that incorruptible life is our accomplishment in the image of God does not mean to say that we are fully finished. We are not like the work of an artist who, after having finished, no longer modifies it. Rather, it seems to me, that immortality is a confirmed way of living up to our creation in the image of God. The life of the Spirit in humanity reaches a point where it can no longer be lost. It is now unhindered, free to continue its progress towards God.

In the end, "when completeness comes, what is in part disappears." (1 Cor 13:10), humans will see the very Lord in whom they have put their hope, their belief here below. They will see their joy, and their joy is the Word made flesh. It is He who, after having 'tabernacled with men' (Dem. 94), will introduce into the company of his Father all those in whom His image is fully restored, in whom His life has penetrated into the depths of their bodies.

We may be disconcerted by the idea that human flesh itself partakes in the incorruptibility of the Uncreated, but it is the scandal of the Cross taken to its ultimate limits. The Word of the Uncreated Father, crucified in His flesh, makes human flesh fit for incorruptible life. It is the light of the Father through Christ's flesh that comes to humans and makes them become His image for life in glory, thus humanity attains incorruptibility invested with the light of the Father. *(See A.H. Bk IV, 20:2..."That the paternal light might meet with and rest upon the flesh of our Lord, and come to us from His resplendent flesh, and that thus man might attain to immortality, having been invested with the paternal light.")* ∎

CHAPTER XI

Yesterday's Questions, Today's Questions

We have followed the articles of the Creed, one after the other, in order to present Irenaeus' faith. Now, to bring this book to a close – not really a conclusion here since it is about life, inexhaustible Life – I would like to return to a theme to which Irenaeus often refers, as we have already seen, the theme of friendship – the human experience of friendship and the friendship between God and humanity.

Are We in a Corrupt World?

In a world perceived as corrupt and hostile, how does one maintain trust in God, how does one believe that God cares about humans? That was the question raised by the Gnostics at the time of Irenaeus. Is not the same question asked by many people today, although in a very different context?

For the Gnostics of the second century, the answer was to push God back into transcendence, that is to say *cut Him off entirely* from the stuff of creation, and then cut oneself off from this same corrupt world in order to ascend towards the ineffable God. In the middle of the second century, this way of seeing this relationship between God and humans had convinced many Christians who were disquieted by the apparent contradiction between divine perfection and the presence of evil in the world.

With a few modifications in the vocabulary and mindsets, these Gnostics of the second century would not be too uncomfortable in one or the other sects or new religions thriving here and there across all continents today, including Europe. Anxiety in the face of the unknown, natural catastrophes, genocides, and disasters caused by human wickedness, go along with a new religious disquiet that drives millions of our contemporaries to seek in the spiritual world what they can no longer find in this world.

In order to fight against the Gnostic dualism of his time, Irenaeus reminded the Christians tempted by these doctrines that the place where the Word became flesh is precisely this world, this world true to the reality in which human beings of flesh and blood live. To do that, he calls upon a whole series of images based on the human experience of friendship. He highlights, as we have seen, the image or signifier of 'accustomization.' He clearly shows that the Word made flesh – Christ, takes the initiative precisely because of His friendship for humanity. If the Word becomes flesh in order to live among humans, it is not out of necessity, for instance, to settle debts, but because of his wish to join the company of his own creatures.

Transformative Friendship

Alluding to Abraham, Irenaeus says: *"Abraham also followed voluntarily and under no compulsion (sine vinculis), because of the noble nature of his faith, and so became the friend of God." (A.H. Bk IV, 13: 4)* Of course, the Abraham figure immediately brings to our mind a promise, that of a posterity and of a land. But, this promise symbolizes an act of trust, of hope without ulterior motives and without calculation. Friendship, when it is genuine, is a grace without right or obligation. For a friend, there is no corner of one's being kept for ourselves alone. Then, in the case of Christ, the Word made flesh within us, the justice brought by His presence drastically changes the entire life of the person who welcomes Him as a friend.

But, to see this through, it must be added that friendship surely does not mean being at peace. The entry of someone else into the life of a human being is rather disruptive. It is an intrusion into what is dear and familiar to us. Because of that, we must transform ourselves, set off on the path again, and set off towards the unknown: "Go from your country, your people," God says to Abraham.

Because this is not a legal requirement but a friend's wish, Abraham can claim no reward, neither land, nor posterity, not even God's friendship as a right. We cannot moralize here about the merits of obedience. The birth of a son from a sterile woman; the sacrifice of his son prevented at the very last moment, Abraham's experience is symbolic of a relationship whose quality can only be appreciated by one single requirement, *to be there*. The discovery of the otherness of the Word made flesh – his intimacy with the Father – transforms the need to possess into the desire to 'see,' that is to say, to know Him as a true person and rejoice in Him as such.

It is this need to 'see' that conveys, in the end, the deep meaning of the coming of the Word on Earth. In one of the rare Irenaean references to the name of Jesus, we read that we received, through Jesus Christ *"the adoption and the inheritance promised to Abraham"*. *(A.H. Bk IV, 8: 1)* The Incarnation is thus perfectly in keeping with the deepest longings of friendship. This means that salvation, the grace of His coming, is to be understood first and foremost in terms of *the fulfillment of a longing* and then, only secondarily, as a response to sin.

Once this has been understood, it is not difficult to grasp the meaning of the various images used by Irenaeus to speak of the proximity of the divine presence, as for instance, the image of 'becoming accustomed to.' These images of the gap between humans and God being filled finally to become a gateway, these images are born of the experience of faith and not of speculative discourse. They explain the human need to get used to others, this because of one's limited nature, one's incapacity to grasp the newness of others unless one takes the time for it.

Christ is the friend who takes time into account, who adjusts to humans and their needs, precisely because of his friendship, a friendship that takes Him to where a human is 'at home.' In fact, it is the same in the case of the divine friend because, Irenaeus says, the Word came 'to His own things.' (*A.H. Bk III, 2: 2*) This is how He fulfills the promise He made to His own that He would live and converse with them on earth.

This image of the divine presence comes from a profound intuition, that which is close to the 'natural desire to see God' as Thomas Aquinas says. If this desire exists in a human heart, in every human heart, it is because the Word is not foreign to the world He created. If the Son has been able to reach the deepest and most inexpressible in human beings in becoming accustomed to the reality of this world, it is because of the friendly complicity of friendship between Himself and humans. And, this friendship goes as far as the *transformative communion.*

Humans Called to the Transformative Union

When friends are together their relationship deepens and tends to become communion. The closer you try to get to someone else, the more you resort to images of intimacy, depth, and transformation to convey the inexpressible nature of the communion that one yearns for. The way the Christian mystics use images of physical love and the most elevated language of love demonstrates a particularly eloquent attempt to use symbols to overcome the inadequacies of human language. *The process of getting to the depths of one's being implies the destruction and wiping out of a previous mindset to arrive at a new level of understanding.* To unite in love, to drink, to eat are human activities through which the meaning of the road taken together, with no possible return, appears more vividly. Somehow these activities hint at the irreversible character of death, but death that symbolically seeks to go beyond the limits of our finite nature and to overcome it so that death becomes new life.

One of the Irenaean images closest to the paradox of death being overcome is that of the *transformative union* brought about by the Eucharist, the flesh is sown with the seed of life, or more exactly with the Sower himself, to set the mortal condition of human beings forever in life. However, humans in the course of their lives before death must be capable of receiving such a gift; Irenaeus says that his *"flesh shall also be found fit for and capable of receiving the power of God". (A.H. Bk V, 3: 2)*

Now, a container is something hollow. In order to receive the gift of life, humans must be hollowed out, purified of everything that would impede the necessary modifications and transformations for union. This brings to mind the idea of longing as a source of suffering as well as a means of bringing about the desired union. He who loves is willing to change his own habits, to transform himself, to get rid of everything that would prevent him from accepting the gift of the other. Thus 'longing,' the work of transformation that becomes active renunciation, makes the union possible.

The dialectics between the longing and the gift is part of a constellation of images in Irenaeus to say that the encounter with the Son overcomes distances and the differences between humans and God. *God yearns for us. This is the most extraordinary assertion of the Christian faith which Irenaeus is continually professing* through images of food, friendship, seed of life, etc. Through symbolic signs of intimacy, he reveals the way by which God comes down to humans, transforms them and makes them capable of bearing His glory.

Of course, this symbolism does not only apply to those nourished with the body of Christ, it also involves all humans nourished by the fruits of creation. If the Son declares the cup and the bread, products of creation to be as His own blood and own body in order to fortify us, He does so because this gesture is highly symbolic for humans: *All, without exception, eat and drink from this same creation.*

If we take this idea a little further, we should say that allowing a human being to starve to death is already a surrender to the powers of death that broke the body and shed the blood of Christ Crucified. In this sense, the Eucharist very clearly symbolizes the necessity of putting the creative forces of humanity to work in order to set up structures capable of resisting the inevitable exploitation of man by man. In the second century, Irenaeus was aware of the extent of human suffering.

What is our awareness in the twenty-first century? Behind all the foodstuffs and things bought every day, how much suffering, how much unseen and well-hidden misery is endured by those who produce these goods in appalling working conditions? Behind the seductive mask of advertising and everything that makes consumption easy, how much injustice and hidden violence is involved in the process of production?

The efforts of some to 'nourish the flesh and blood' of the starved and the exploited, the Son has made them His by attesting the worth of the creation by a gift of Himself which took Him to transfigured death. "Truly, truly, I say to you, unless a grain of wheat falls into the earth and dies, it remains alone; but if it dies, it bears much fruit." (Jn 12:24)

Here is what Irenaeus says about food, the body and the Eucharist:

"...that dispensation (by which the Lord became) an actual man, consisting of flesh, and nerves, and bones – that (flesh) which is nourished by the cup which is His blood, and receives increase from the bread which is His body. And just as a cutting from the vine planted in the ground fructifies in its season, or as a grain of wheat falling into the earth (Jn 12:24) and becoming decomposed, rises with manifold increase by the Spirit of God, who contains all things, and then, through the wisdom of God, serves for the use of men, and having received the Word of God, becomes the Eucharist, which is the body and blood of Christ; so also our bodies, being nourished by it, and deposited in the earth, and suffering decomposition there, shall rise at their appointed time, the Word of God granting them resurrection to the glory of God, even the Father, who freely gives to this mortal immortality, and to this corruptible incorruption, because the strength of God is made perfect in weakness." (A.H. Bk V, 2: 3) ■

THE TRANSLATORS' JOURNEY
by
DANIELLE GAGNEUR
AND
THOMAS THOMSON

THOUGH AMERICAN, DONNA SINGLES WROTE IN FRENCH BECAUSE she was teaching in France, hence the necessity to translate her book from French into English – and American English no less – as we went through the process of editing the book with the Sisters of Saint Joseph, the now famous GREM group – Grace, Renee, Elizabeth, and Mila! The principle that has guided us is to *be true to Donna's work.* Translating is a process that often leaves translators with the acute awareness that "to translate is to betray," hence our need to address the questions that were raised during this journey from French into English. We hope that our explanations here will serve to help the reader reach a better understanding of Donna Singles' work.

A.) WHY NOT 'MAN' OR 'HUMAN' IN THE TITLE?

Donna Singles' book was originally published under the title *L'homme debout,* literally *the standing man* or *the man who stands.* Thus, why not use *man* or *human* in the title?

Though our immediate reaction was to use the word *man* in order to translate *homme,* we gradually became aware of the gender issue surrounding the use of the term *man* in the USA today. We became more and more sensitive to the real difference between the use of the word *homme* in France and that of *man* in the UK, and of *man* or *human* in the USA, as well as the different usages depending on the public in the USA. We also became more aware of the changes currently taking place in both English and French.

In France, the word *homme* is more immediately understood in the generic sense than the word *man* is in America. For instance, we refer to *la déclaration des droits de l'homme* instead of *the declaration of human rights* (droits humains). Yet, in Switzerland it would be totally inappropriate to refer in French to *la déclaration des droits de l'homme*. They refer to *La Déclaration des droits humains*.

Donna Singles was living in France and wrote in French. She thus used the French language with the specificity that we have just mentioned. She used the word *homme* found in the sources at her disposal. This concerned quotes from the Bible, from Irenaeus' books translated into French, and the language used by French theologians of her time. She therefore used the word *homme* as a matter a course.

We decided to make a close study of the way the word *man* was used by Donna Singles in this book. The word *man* occurs more than 600 times. And looking into the use of the word turns out to be very enlightening.

The first time that Donna Singles uses the word *homme* (man), or rather, to be more precise the first time that she could have used the word *homme,* she does not do so. She uses the words *être humain* (human being) instead. And yet, she refers to Christ who was indeed a man and this is striking as the reader might have expected to read the word *man* rather than *human being.* The reason is that she is addressing the issue of resurrection, and she thinks from a theologian's point of view.

"Today, we find it very difficult to conceive the degree of incredulity but also of hope aroused by the idea that God had raised a <u>human being</u> from the dead (P. 21). (Nous avons beaucoup de mal aujourd' hui à imaginer l'incrédulité mais aussi l'espérance qu' avait suscitées l'idée que Dieu avait ressuscité <u>un être humain.</u> (P. 18. French Edition).

As a theologian she rightly saw the importance of referring to Christ as a human being, particularly when dealing with resurrection. It is, in our eyes, a very significant choice. It echoes Paul's words in Galatians: "There is no longer Jew or Gentile, slave or free, male and female. For you are all one in Christ Jesus," (il n'y a plus ni homme ni femme." Galates 3 :28)

Moving forward in our study we observe that the major theological issues of incarnation and recapitulation are also addressed with the same attentiveness. Referring to incarnation through the theme of *accustomization*, Donna Singles uses the word *homme,* but she develops this notion using the words *genre humain* (human race) (P. 56) *"The Spirit has accustomed the Son to dwell in the <u>human </u>race." (L'Esprit a accoutumé le Fils à habiter dans le genre<u> humain.</u> P. 47, French edition)*

This concern for the human dimension is equally to be found when tackling the notion of *recapitulation.* The terminology used is that of *humanité* (humanity/humankind) instead of *man,* to stress of course, the theological point that Christ has come to save all humankind.

The word *humanité* occurs four times in Chapter IV, P. 74-75, French edition:

1) *"How could humankind following in Adam's footsteps be saved?" (P. 88). (Comment l'humanité qui se situe dans le sillage d'Adam pouvait-elle être sauvée? P. 74 French edition).*

2) *"The first...launched humankind on the path of sin and death." (P. 88). (Le premier...a lancé l'humanité sur le chemin du péché et de la mort. P. 74 French edition).*

3) *"His gift for encompassing the whole of humanity..." (P. 88). (Son habitude de saisir l'humanité entière... P. 74. French edition)*

4) *"He encompasses all humanity." (P. 89). ("Il touche l'humanité entière," P. 75, French edition).*

It is striking to note that on one particular occasion, when using the word *homme*, she is careful to attract the reader's attention to the correct understanding of the word *homme* in the generic sense. She does so by adding the word *anthropos* in parenthesis *"La perte est au niveau de l'homme (anthropos) (P. 75 French edition); The loss concerns the human being (anthropos)." (P. 89)* One must bear in mind that *anthropos* is the Greek word for *man* in the generic sense as opposed to *andros* referring to *male*.

So, as far as such central notions as resurrection, incarnation, and recapitulation are concerned, Donna Singles' vocabulary is not limited to the word *homme* (man). She clearly stresses the broad human dimension by resorting to a more inclusive terminology.

Thus, Donna Singles wrote as a theologian but her use of the French language may also have been influenced by the specificity of English, her native language.

Looking into quotes from *Against Heresies* and *Demonstration of the Apostolic Preaching* reveals that the word *man* in English is less extensively used than the word *homme* in French. The translator has therefore used *human being* instead. The English and French translations of the same original text of Irenaeus testify to this difference between the two languages. The Latin word *hominum* is translated to *human beings* in English and *hommes* in French in the following quote about recapitulation, "When He became incarnate and was made man, He commenced afresh the long line of <u>human beings</u>." *(P. 89) (A.H. Bk III, 18:1-2)*, *("Lorsqu'il s'est incarné et s'est fait homme, il a récapitulé en lui – même la longue histoire des <u>hommes</u>." P. 75, French edition)* In fact, Donna Singles drew upon this difference when dealing with the theme of accustomization: "The Spirit has accustomed the Son to dwell in the human race," is derived from *Against Heresies*, "He made the Son of man, becoming accustomed…to dwell in the human race, to rest with <u>human beings</u>," *(Il s'accoutumait à habiter dans le genre humain." A.H BK. III, 17)*

But the difference does not lie exclusively between English and French. There is a change in the acceptance of the word *man* nowadays that affects the translation of the Bible itself. This is essential for us in Genesis 1:26. Here are three examples:

1) King James version: "Let us make man in our image."

2) New International Version: "Let us make mankind in our image, in our likeness."

3) New Living Translation: "Let us make human beings in our image, to be like us."

Donna Singles used the standard quote in French similar to King James, *"Faisons l'homme à notre image,"* as this change has not yet affected the most famous French translations of the Bible. She thus used the word *homme,* but immediately commented on its meaning by using the word *humanité.* "The call for being in the image and likeness means that, from the start, humankind was defined in terms of a vocation." *(L'appel à l'image et à la ressemblance veut dire que dès le début l'humanité a été définie en terme de vocation.)* She also uses the word *humanité* when developing the theme of the hands of God by quoting from *Demonstration of the Apostolic Preaching.* The word *homme* (man) is within the quote, "man he formed with his own hands" (Dem 11. P. 36 French edition), but she makes it very clear that "creation is meant to be for the salvation of humanity," *(P. 32) (la création est au service du salut de l'humanité, P. 27, French edition)* It is clear that Donna Singles quoted from texts as they existed and commented by frequently using a more inclusive terminology.

Things are changing today, especially in the USA, and this raises a question for our translation. The most famous and widely-known French translations of the Bible have not yet changed the word *homme* into *être humain* [28] as is the case in the English language. However, some translations no longer refer to *homme* but instead to *Adam* [29] or the *glèbeux* [30] (the earthling). According to etymology [31] *Adam* means *man* and *mankind/humankind.* Donna Singles clearly refers to "Adam as humankind," *(Adam signifiant de l'humanité. P. 67, French edition).* Adam is also related to the Hebrew *adamah,* understood as *le terreux,* the earthling. In that respect, it is interesting to note that in the Latin version of *Against Heresies,* Book II, the Greek word *protoplasto* is translated into English as *first-formed man* and in French as *premier homme.* Yet, protoplasto only refers to "the first formed" in Greek with no explicit reference

---

28 Though various French studies use the word *humain* in the translation of Genesis 1:26. For example:

a) Article by Patrice Rolin, from « Un mot de la Bible », Fréquence protestante, 100.7 FM du 2 septembre 2006

b) *La Divine Origine, Dieu n'a pas crée l'homme,* Marie Balmary, Ed; Grasset, 1982

29 «Dieu dit /Faisons un adam/ à notre image ». La bible Paris /Montréal. Bayard/ Médiaspaul. 2001

30 "Nous ferons Adâm le Glébeux à notre réplique, selon notre ressemblance » La Bible André Chouraqui 1987/2010.

31 www.universalis.fr/encyclopedie/adam/ – from Barim Publications' Online Dictionary of Biblical Hebrew

to "man." (*Protoplasto* is Πρωτόςπλαοτος in Greek and means *first formed.*)

So, for the translators, the question remains, what would Donna Singles write today were she able to translate her own French version into English? There is and there will be no definitive answer to this question. Yet it seems to us, that in American English today, she would be attentive to use gender-inclusive language.

We have pointed out how she already used in French an inclusive terminology concerning major theological points. We have seen the way she constantly draws our attention to the generic human dimension when commenting upon quotes using the terms *homme*. In fact, *humanité* (humanity/humankind) is a key word in her writing. This is also to be found in the central notion that Christ is "the principle of humanity," *(P. 101) ("Christ principe de l'humanité," P. 84, French Edition).*

We think that, writing in English today, she would be keen to use the *New Living Translation* of Genesis 1:26 (NLT): "Let us make human beings in our image," for which there is not yet any equivalent in widely-known French translations. This quote is all the more important as it is closely related to the notion that triggered Donna Singles' life-long interest and study of Irenaeus, "the vocation of human beings is inscribed in their flesh." This NLT translation has been most influential in our thinking. We decided to revise our initial translation based on the assumption that *Man*, with a capital letter, was the way to refer to humankind in the generic sense, as we were first told by a British editor. It may still work in UK for some. It does not seem to suit American English usage today.

Of course, we did not alter the word *man* in the quotations, but we have chosen a gender-inclusive language to translate Donna Singles' text from French into English. By doing so we feel we are moving forward in the direction she herself indicated when she chose to write in French as a theologian.

As for the title, we did not want it to be the flagship of any gender language controversy. Ultimately, we came to the conclusion that, the imperative form, *stand up*, is the best answer as it is inclusive, regardless of any particular sensitivity to the use of *man* or *human*. It addresses us all.

Stand Up

The image *debout* (stand/standup) is so significant in Irenaeus that Donna Singles wrote a whole chapter entitled "L'homme debout" in her doctoral thesis. [32] Thus she demonstrates how central this notion is.

Of course, as is usual with Irenaeus, this image is not to be understood on the physical level but as an image of faith, of life, and not of any life, but the life of resurrection and life with God. Attentive readers will notice this wording in chapter V. The word *debout* occurs 6 times on page 83 (French edition). "Christ makes his disciples *stand up* to face life, and *stand* in this world as if already resurrected. Finally, Christ makes the dead *stand up* by bringing them the good news of their resurrection." Developing the way Irenaeus uses symbolic language to help people understand faith, Donna stresses the meaning of this image in three cases, at the last supper, in the garden, and when descending to the dead.

1) "During the Last Supper, the Lord gives the bread of life to his <u>recumbent</u> disciples, because of their need for food

---

32 "Le salut de l'homme chez saint Irénée. Essai d'interprétation symbolique" Chapter V: *L'Homme Debout*, P. 236

which was not only physical but spiritual. *(P. 100/P. 83 French edition)*

2)　"Lying on the ground in the garden... But they are not left sleeping because the Lord awakens them and makes them *stand up.*" *(P. 99/P.82-83 French edition)*

3)　Irenaeus explains that Christ, in this way, indicates the fruit of his suffering: the awakening of humanity after the sleep of death, its being made to *stand up* by the resurrection." *(P. 99/ P. 82-83, French edition)*

BECOMING FULLY ALIVE

Donna Singles makes a clear connection between "standing up" and being "fully alive." The previously cited quote goes on: *"This is perfectly in keeping with Irenaeus' idea that 'human beings fully alive' are essentially 'human beings standing up," humans awakened and nourished by the Lord so that they might set themselves on the path to neverending life."* *(P. 99/P. 83, French edition)*

"*Standing up* starts a process as humans…set themselves on the path to never-ending life." It is this process of 'becoming fully alive' that she develops throughout her book to present Irenaeus' faith and theology. *Stand up* is a powerful image to convey and introduce the path to this never-ending process of becoming.

"Fully Alive" points to Irenaeus' central vision and evokes a famous quote, which everyone has in mind when referring to Irenaeus, even if it has often been truncated, "The Glory of God is Man Fully Alive and the life of Man is the vision of God."

B) "Man Fully Alive" or "A Living Man"?

In order to translate the French quote in the preface and in the last subtitle of Chapter X, we expected to read the following from our English source, "The glory of God is man fully alive and the life of man is the vision of God." Yet, we became aware that there are two English translations for the French quote. *Man fully alive* or *a living man* for *homme vivant*. The accepted translation today seems to be *Man fully alive*. It has even become so commonplace that it is to be found in the *Catholic Catechism* (article 294). It is also the English translation of the address given by John Paul II at the Catholic University of Lyon during his third visit there in 1986. Our English Source of *Against Heresies* is slightly different and is a literal translation: "The glory of God is a living man; and the life of man consists in beholding God." Which one is the most appropriate? We finally decided to use both depending on the context.

In Chapter X, it was important for us to refer to the literal quote (P. 176) from our English source referring to A.H. Bk IV, 20:7. The main reason is that it is closer to both the Latin *vivens homo* and the Greek *zôn anthropos*. We chose to use *a living man*, though the whole quote is less elegant and concise. But in our eyes, our choice does not undermine the relevance of the current translation *fully alive*. This is why we have made a different choice for the preface. There, Ingmar Granstedt introduces the book by using everyday language and without any specific reference to the quote from *Against Heresies*. This is why, after checking with him and with his consent, we decided to translate the French to the popular English quote most known today. (P. 12)

It is interesting to note the link that Donna Singles makes between the two notions. For Irenaeus, to be *alive* is to be *fully alive*. She writes: "Human beings will be perfectly in the likeness of their creator once they have reached full maturity, becoming incarnate spirits who are *living humans* in the full sense of the words *humans fully alive* (P. 104, French edition). *"L'homme ressemblera parfaitement à son créateur lorsqu'il aura atteint pleinement sa stature d'homme, esprit incarné, devenu "homme vivant" au sens plein du mot."*) This brings us to the issue of Greek and Latin.

C) What About Greek and Latin?

Irenaeus' text in Greek, Latin, and Armenian.

The reader must bear in mind that Irenaeus wrote in Greek and we only have access to the full text of *Against Heresies* in Latin and Armenian. The Greek text is very incomplete. Right from the start, translation has been an unavoidable process to reach Irenaeus since both Latin and Armenian are translations from the original Greek. Our journey from French into English is in fact the follow up of a journey initiated from the Greek onwards. Of course, in order to be true to Irenaeus, we did not translate the quotes from *Against Heresies* from French into English, but we resorted to the English translation [33] done directly from Latin or Greek. To do otherwise would have been a source of many potential errors.

Can Greek or Latin help?

It is to be noted that, on some rare occasions, the French and the English translations made from Greek and Latin happen to

---

33 English translation: *Against Heresies* (St. Irenaeus) Fathers of the Church www.newadvent.org, Translated by Alexander Roberts and William Rambaut. From Ante-Nicene Fathers, Vol. 1. Edited by Alexander Roberts, James Donaldson, and A. Cleveland Coxe. (Buffalo, NY: Christian Literature Publishing Co., 1885.) Revised and edited for *New Advent* by Kevin Knight, www.newadvent.org.

differ somewhat. This is why going back to the Latin and Greek has sometimes been necessary and helpful when trying to be faithful to Donna's text. Let us take two examples.

1. The first one is taken from Chapter IX dealing with the *unfinished nature of Man. (Footnote 26, page 160)*

Irenaeus refers to Adam who disobeyed. The French translation explicitly states *non par malice,* that is to say *not out of wickedness,* whereas the English does not make this lack of wickedness explicit. It even seems, at first, to point to the opposite meaning, though the text in parentheses is not very clear in the following: "still wickedly (on the part of the other)." This is why we had to check the text both in Latin and Greek.

Another difference is to be noted between the Latin and the Greek texts and this might be the reason for the different translations in English and in French. The Latin [*sed 'male'*] does not use a negation before *male,* whereas the Greek text is perfectly clear about man's lack of wickedness, all *akakôs* (but innocent). The French translation is thus, for us, clearly confirmed by the Greek. The reader must bear in mind that the Latin text is itself a translation from the original Greek. This is why we changed the ambiguous English translation. We did this in order to be faithful to Donna's quote from the French translation by Rousseau [34] in which Adam disobeyed "par inadvertence et non par malice," that is to say, "inadvertently and not out of wickedness."

Our translation is also consistent with Irenaeus' view of Adam, which is quite different from that of Augustine. For Irenaeus,

---

34 Donna Singles used the French translation from: *Contre les hérésies (Contre les hérésies. Dénonciation et réfutation de la prétendue gnose au nom menteur,* traduc-

incarnation is not primarily due to Adam's disobedience. It is part of the original design.

2. The second example is to be found in Chapter II, *creation is an unfinished symphony. (Footnote 10, page 35)*

We are told that Irenaeus was so convinced of the presence of God in the world that he saw the whole creation under the sign of the Cross. Donna Singles' assertion is based on a quote from *Against Heresies*, which clearly mentions the cross in French *"au plan invisible il soutenait toutes les choses créées et se trouvait imprimé [ou enfoncé] en forme de croix dans la Création entière." (P. 29, French edition)*

The English translation from which we take our quotes does not mention the Cross, "God...in an invisible manner contains all things created, and is inherent in the entire creation..." To stick to this English translation would have made Donna Singles' paragraph and reasoning inconsistent, so we checked the quote from *Against Heresies* as translated from Greek and Latin by Adelin Rousseau and discovered a six-page long footnote(!) in which the translator explains his choice of the image of the cross. His choice was based on an analysis of the text in three languages: Greek, Latin, and Armenian, as well as the immediate context, and the context of T*he Demonstration of the Apostolic Tradition*: "In it is crucified the Son of God, inscribed crosswise upon it all..." (Dem.34) So, in order to be true to the French translation used by Donna Singles, we slightly modified the English translation by adding the image of the cross, "inscribed in the shape of a cross [or inherent] in the entire creation..."

Yet, it is to be noted that in the new edition revised in 1991, the same translator chose to translate "se trouvait enfoncé dans la Création entière..." Donna was very careful to be precise.

---

tion Fse Adelin Rousseau, Paris, Ed. du Cerf, 1991.

Although her point relies on the first version, she also refers to the subsequent version in parentheses: (*ou enfoncé*), which also matches the English version translated by Alexander Roberts and William Rambaut. Accordingly, our translation takes the two versions into account.

D) Flesh, Body, or Dead?

A last question may be worthy of attention. Donna's book is structured along the lines of the articles of the *Creed, The Apostles' Creed,* the short *Creed* currently used at Mass. The title of Chapter X is, "I believe in the resurrection of the flesh." The word *flesh* raises a question for the translators. Today the words used in the *Creed* are "I believe in the resurrection of the body." Since 2010, *The Apostles' Creed* has been modified thus in the Catholic liturgy according to the third edition of the *Roman Missal.*

Should we say, "I believe in the resurrection of the flesh," "the resurrection of the body," or the "resurrection of the dead?" Our choice has been to refer to the resurrection of 'the flesh.' We have done so because Donna used the word "chair" (*flesh*) and so did Irenaeus as shown in Chapter X dealing with this article of faith. There is no set phrase in *Against Heresies* for the literal wording, "I believe in the resurrection of the flesh," but Donna Singles tells us that "Irenaeus speaks at length of the incorruptibility of the flesh – of its resurrection, and of its everlasting life after death." She refers to "the flesh possessed by the Spirit." She reminds us of the historical reason, the need for Irenaeus to refute the Gnostics who despised both body and flesh. Another possibility could have been, "I believe in the resurrection of the dead," as it is to be found in the *Nicene Creed* but Donna clearly refers to the *Apostles' Creed* at the beginning of her book.

Donna Singles wrote her book in 2005, that is to say, before the change in the Catholic missal and the wording of the *Apostles' Creed*. What word would she use today, *flesh* or *body*? Either flesh or body would do, since Irenaeus used both, *"our bodies...shall rise at their appointed time..." (A.H. Bk V, 2:3)*. Donna would also probably remind us that "Irenaeus uses symbolic language...He knows very well there is no image to convey adequately our hope of resurrection." *(P 82, French Edition)*

This change in the choice of words points to a never-ending process that is at work both in translation and within each language.

E) A Neverending Process, A Creative Process, and an Experience

We probably do not need any more examples to become aware of a process that goes beyond the task of translating from one language into another and that also affects every language in its own necessary evolution.

The issue at stake is that of language itself and the way it relates to the reality that it tries to convey: a reality that changes as our understanding of that same reality changes. Examples would abound of the necessity to adapt words in different places at different times in order to make sense to people. Words change with time. For instance, the phrase "the Holy Ghost" has become today "the Holy Spirit."

The use of the word man is another telling example. We went through a series of potential titles such as: *Man Fully Alive, The Human Fully Alive, The Human Stand Up,* before choosing *Stand Up, Becoming Fully Alive.*

The issue of language is thus a crucial one, but beyond language, something else is at work. In her final chapter, Donna raises questions related to present day issues. She was acutely aware of the part played by language. She writes, "Is it also a language that can speak to Christians in our century? The images of the *Creed* have remained unchanged to the present day: 'descent to the dead', 'on the third day', 'resurrection of the flesh.' I think that Irenaeus' approach, if not his language, is highly instructive as it shows us how important it is to go beyond the literal meaning of words in order to access their deeper meaning. It is the symbolic dimension that is at work here – the same as in the sacraments." (*P. 85, L'homme debout*) One cannot help thinking here of "the Word made flesh," of how words relate to reality and especially of how the "Word" relates to our own lives.

Translating this book has been a creative process involving language, words, and people, especially a wonderful six-person editing team. It has been a true experience of friendship and love. This creative process has made us feel deeply how Donna Singles has been and is still with us today through her presentation of Irenaeus' faith. Today, she is for us truly and really "Fully Alive."

Danielle GAGNEUR, Thomas THOMSON

ABOUT DONNA SINGLES

Photo courtesy of Keith De Cesare

Donna Singles was born in 1928 in Grand Rapids, Michigan USA. She died in 2005 in Traverse City, Michigan, just back from Lyon. She entered the Congregation of the Sisters of Saint Joseph when she was twenty and then became a teacher in their schools. In 1967, she came to France to study theology at the Catholic University of Lyon, which led to her doctoral thesis, "Le Salut de l'homme chez saint Irénée. Essai d'interprétation symbolique." (The Salvation of Humanity According to Saint Irenaeus: A Study in Symbolic Interpretation.) She stayed in this university where she then became a full member of the teaching staff. She lectured on Irenaeus, of course, but also conducted study groups and courses on the Eucharist, ministry and hope, as well as an important movement, though little known in France, referred to as "Process Theology" – a way of conceiving God as continuously becoming.

Donna Singles came to Lyon from the USA, her native land, and it was in Lyon, the capital of the Gauls, that Irenaeus settled after leaving Smyrna, his native town (now Izmir in Turkey). Their similar faiths met across the centuries, thus spurring for years the considerable energy and enthusiasm of this exceptional American woman. Donna was passionate about Irenaeus' clear and positive spirit in the midst of the Gnostic heresies that were unfolding at the time of the Early

Church. She wanted to convey how relevant Irenaeus' faith can be to-day.

According to Saint Irenaeus, the vocation of human beings is inscribed in their flesh, fashioned in God's image. For Donna Singles, who at the time was a student of theology in Lyon, that statement came as a real shock when she heard it pronounced by Professor Maurice Jourjon. Eighteen centuries lie between, yet the thoughts of Irenaeus are so close to the sources of the Christian faith that they can still speak to men and women of our time through his joyful vision of the advent of Christ, his view of life as a growing process and his call upon us to participate in the unfinished symphony of creation.

Combining passion with precision and the mastery born of her long studies of Irenaeus' work, Donna offers us here her 'key for reading,' a reader's guide to access his language which is that of the early centuries, in order to discover how clearly he can speak to us and enlighten our lives today. The chapters of the book quite simply follow the articles of the Creed, the Apostles' Creed, Irenaeus' own faith being utilized as a way of throwing light on each of the articles. This provides a particularly clear and accessible presentation.

BOOK REVIEW

Source : Theophilyon, Tome 15,volume 2, 2010
Donna Singles: *l'Homme debout. Le credo de saint Irénée*, **Préf. Ingmar Granstedt, Paris, Cerf, 2008, 159p.**

A US citizen and theology student who became a theology professor at the Catholic University of Lyon, the author found there a place conducive to the study of Irenaeus, the second bishop of the city. We must bear in mind the teaching of Maurice Jourjon there with the publication of both *Against Heresies* and the *Demonstration of the Apostolic Preaching* by *Sources Chrétiennes.*

Donna Singles made the study of Irenaeus her own, as demonstrated by her thesis at the beginning of the 1970s, *Le Salut de l'homme chez Saint Irénée. Essai d'interprétation symbolique. (Man's salvation according to Saint Irenaeus: a study in Symbolic Interpretation.)* With Jean Comby, in 2005 she published an anthology *La Gloire de Dieu, c'est l'homme vivant, (The Glory of God is Man Fully Alive.)* It was widely read. Her personal papers would provide further evidence of her great knowledge and command in her field. All this gives great weight to this little posthumous volume that we owe to the faithful and careful editing of a former colleague and friend, who wrote the preface. The author has a thorough knowledge of this Church father. This is the first reason for reading and studying *l'Homme debout.*

Astoundingly realistic and optimistic writings come to the fore. The clarity of the presentation is a second asset with its punchy sentences and conclusive summaries for nearly every chapter. A clear outline is provided by the use of the Creed. (She takes the articles of the Creed one by one to show the way Irenaeus understood them. A chapter is devoted to each article.) This use of the Creed is undoubtedly anachronistic, since Irenaeus did not have this Creed at hand at the time, in the same way as Origen only had the basics of the faith. Donna Singles knew this very well as her anthology testifies. It is a pedagogic choice to awaken shared beliefs and to engage in a sort of hand-to-hand fight between what Irenaeus says and what we say because we have to say it. Irenaeus fights the good fight.

What matters most is what makes him topical and hence still relevant today. Basically, Irenaeus' anthropology appears to be extremely innovative and fruitful. Life is the dominant theme, first for man and then for the world around him. Life is seen as a process of growth and that is the point. Evil, the Fall, and Redemption, in no way minimized or reduced to myth disconnected from reality, are part of this growth, which is a gift. And to see life in this way is already a gift, *the* gift.

This is the way the two dimensions of Christian theology in its twofold aspect, the Divine and the Divine-Human in Christ are brought together in an enlivening union as we can see in the first two articles, Chapter 2 and 3, "I believe in God, the Father Almighty, Creator of heaven and earth," "I believe in Jesus Christ, His only Son, our lord, who was conceived by the Holy Spirit, born of the Virgin Mary." It is a theology of God's Design, but not as a reality to be learned in addition to the reality of life. It is life itself in its growth from protology to eschatology.

What is good for the world is for man to acknowledge this by calling God his Father and Creator. What is bad for the world is for man to reject this.

Salvation is that, in his fullness, God Himself, by His Word and his Son, recreates reasoned and filial unity for the benefit of humankind. After the opening chapters, the ones that follow only serve to drive home the same point through each article of the Creed, the Last Judgment, the Holy Spirit, the Church, the remission of sins and the resurrection of the flesh.
It is quite remarkable to notice that all of Irenaeus' thinking is summed up in the quotation which is so popular nowadays and for which he is so famous. All of Irenaeus' *anthropotheology* lies in "the Glory of God is Man Fully Alive and the life of man is the vision of God." This is Donna Singles' conclusion, but she had first to make it clear through each of the articles of the Creed.

Where does the innovative strength of these assertions come from? The author reminds us of this over and over again. Certainly not from the Gnostic danger, with its radical dualism of the spirit and the flesh instilled in the interpretation of the Bible. The Holy Scriptures have nothing to do with this deadly divide, which they contradict. The other anti-Gnostic theologians (Tertullian, Clement, Origen, Theophilus) were as forcefully reactive as Irenaeus was.
Where does Irenaeus's topicality and relevance lie? Not so much in his denunciation as in his assertion. The denunciation of legalism, moralism,

Augustinism, and Papism, was fierce in the aftermath of May 1968 with all its excesses. In fact these may be discarded as unimportant, though they do serve to highlight a threat. But where the rampant threat of Gnostic dualism still persists in all these trends as in many others, the assertion of grace by Irenaeus continues and will continue to play a part. No doubt this grace inspired Donna Singles when writing her book, *l'homme Debout*.

by Dominique Bertrand

(Review translated into English by
Danielle Gagneur and Thomas Thomson)

Theophilyon is a publication indexed in the ATLA religion Database of the American Theological Library Association
300 S. Walker Dr., Suite 2100, Chicago, IL 60606 USA
Email: atla@atla.com   Website: www.atla.com

ATLA Religion Database® (ATLA RDB®)

The *ATLA Religion Database®* (*ATLA RDB®*) is the premier index to journal articles, book reviews, and collections of essays in all fields of religion, with coverage from 1949 and retrospective indexing for some journal issues as far back as the nineteenth century. Journals are selected for inclusion according to their scholarly merit and scope. The fact that many publishers solicit the inclusion of their journals in *ATLA RDB* is indicative of the stature it has achieved in the community of religion scholars.